Praise for
God Alone Is Enough

"Reading *God Alone Is Enough* was an absolute joy . . . I experienced it as the gift of two older, sassy, rib-tickling sisters—one Teresa of Avila and the other Claudia of Burney—who sat their kid brother (me) up on the washing machine and said, 'Look, junior, this is what love is all about.' You trust them because you believe they care for you, but moreover because they have that glorious foolishness in their eyes."

—JOHN BLASE, author of
Touching Wonder: Recapturing the Awe of Christmas

"This is the kind of book that a serious Christian has to thank God for. It only illuminates and opens St. Teresa of Avila in a profound and intimate way. I cannot recommend this book too highly or, I suspect, even adequately. Read it and you will see what I mean."

—PHYLLIS TICKLE, author of *The Divine Hours*

"A refreshing and engaging exploration with Teresa of Avila. Also, a true journey of soul into the heart of prayer."

—VINITA HAMPTON WRIGHT, author of *Dwelling Places*

"I've been waiting for some time for the Ragamuffin Diva to write us a book about her own spiritual quest. And what she has delivered in *God Alone Is Enough* is beautifully written, winsome, and touching. Hers is a voice to which we all should listen. And the fact that she brings Teresa of Avila right into our own backyards makes it even better."

—TONY JONES, author of many books, including
The Teaching of the Twelve: Believing and Practicing the Primitive Christianity of the Ancient Didache Community

"Claudia Mair Burney writes with courage and compassion, capturing the best of Teresa and offering it to her readers with clarity and humor. *God Alone Is Enough* is an invitation and a celebration. Expect to swoon, prepare to feast."

—JENNY SCHROEDEL, author of *Naming the Child*

"I can hardly wait to give copies of this book to everyone I know. She does a beautiful job of showing us the humanity of someone we've long placed on a pedestal, while pointing us toward the trail blazed for us by Teresa of Avila's utter devotion to God. This is an absolute treasure of spiritual writing."

—JANELLE C. SCHNEIDER, author and spiritual director

God Alone Is Enough

a *Spirited Journey with*
St. Teresa of Avila

CLAUDIA MAIR BURNEY

PARACLETE PRESS
BREWSTER, MASSACHUSETTS

God Alone Is Enough: A Spirited Journey with St. Teresa of Avila

2010   First Printing

Copyright © 2010 by Claudia Mair Burney

ISBN: 978-1-55725-661-4

Unless otherwise indicated, Scripture quotations are taken from THE MESSAGE. Copyright © 1993, 1994, 1995, 1996, 2000, 2001, 2002. Used by permission of NavPress Publishing Group.

Scriptures marked (RSV) are taken from the *Revised Standard Version of the Bible* Copyright © 1946, 1952, 1971, by the Division of Christian Education, of the National Council of Churches of Christ in the USA, used by permission.

The Ecstasy of St. Teresa by Gian Lorenzo Bernini (1645-52), Cappella Cornaro, Santa Maria della Vittoria, Rome. Photograph by Marie-Lan Nguyen. All rights reserved.

Library of Congress Cataloging-in-Publication Data

Burney, Claudia Mair, 1964-
  God alone is enough : a spirited journey with St. Teresa of Avila / Claudia Mair Burney.
     p. cm.
  Includes bibliographical references.
  ISBN 978-1-55725-661-4
  1. Teresa, of Avila, Saint, 1515-1582. 2. Spiritual life--Catholic Church. 3. Spirituality--Catholic Church. I. Title.
  BX4700.T4B88 2010
  248.4'82--dc22   2010006552

10 9 8 7 6 5 4 3 2 1

Published by Paraclete Press
Brewster, Massachusetts
www.paracletepress.com

Printed in the United States of America

To Terry Behimer, my soul friend

I have found nothing that compares to the magnificent beauty
of a soul, and its marvelous magnitude.
—Teresa of Avila

Contents

It's silly to think that my words could be meaningful to anyone other than my friends, but if one person reads this and praises my Beloved a little more, God will be granting me a great favor. He knows I'm not interested in anything else. If I manage to say something well, my friends understand that this doesn't come from me; there would be no foundation for it unless the

Lord gives it to me! If they're wrong about this, it will be because they're as ignorant as I am incapable. Only God in his mercy gives such things to us.

—St. Teresa of Avila

Author's Note

Don't call me a saint. I don't want to be dismissed that easily.
—Dorothy Day

When I was a little girl my mother bought me a silver Virgin Mary necklace. I was in love with the tiny Our Lady of Lourdes charm, but she was an anomaly in my otherwise saint-free childhood. As a teen I came to believe a saint was a deeply devout and very much alive person, like the old church mothers who sat near the altar in my congregation, crying out joyful or plaintive hallelujahs. If I was a good girl, and occasionally I was, I too was a saint.

By this time I'd learned other spiritual traditions honored the godly dead who had led exemplary lives. The prefix "St." preceded the names of these special people. Unfortunately, I'd been taught not to trust those sacred traditions, so I missed out on the immense treasures the officially canonized had to offer.

I understand the kind of skittishness some people will bring to this book. Not everyone grew up regaled by inspiring—and sometimes gruesome—saint stories. There were no icons on their walls opening windows to heaven. No plaster statue of the Virgin Mary stood like a serene sentry on their chest of drawers. There wasn't even a blissful, concrete St. Francis of Assisi—complete with birds perched on his shoulders—poised

xii God Alone Is Enough

in their garden. To them the esteemed dead in Christ are gone for heaven's sake. Literally. They're gone for heaven's sake, and accoutrements of devotion to saints such as medals, holy cards, and candles are at best extrabiblical, or downright superstitious. Yet other readers who pick up this book will love the saints, and find those same things to be sacramentals, visible signs that draw them closer to God, and sanctify all areas of their lives.

We won't get into any of that here.

Instead, I'd like for the saint-skeptical among us to reimagine what a saint is, and for our purposes here, consider those dear souls to be friends in high places. Think of this book as an invitation for you to get to know a reliable ally, St. Teresa of Avila, who has already walked, ran, and sometimes inched, baby step by baby step, into the arms of God. A journey is so much more enjoyable when you share it with someone who's already traveled the road you're on, and St. Teresa is much safer than a person you could meet online or speed-dating.

I've gently paraphrased and condensed her words for this trip, but I encourage you to pick up her books and read them for yourself. They're as remarkable as she is. Let this book simply serve as a disarming introduction to her teachings.

With that said, let's meet our illustrious guide for this pilgrimage. We're going to have a grand adventure.

An Opening Prayer
by St. Teresa of Avila

From silly devotions and sullen saints
deliver me, O Lord! Amen.

Introduction
My Invitation and Yours

Winter always calls on me in the middle of August. It's just a whisper of the season, an unmistakable chill slashing like a knife through the heat, but its cold breath never fails to startle me. Despite my ardent desire to remain in denial, I brace myself. Soon the temperature will drop. The leaves will brown on their solemn branches and my mood will nosedive. Before the end of November I'll be trapped in an inner terrain akin to Dante's third circle of hell, where the poor souls are forced to lie in a loathsome slush made of black snow, glacial rain, and battering hail.

Doctors call what I experience seasonal affective disorder, or SAD. To me it feels like hypothermia of the soul. The wretched scourge freezes me in place, usually in my bed, until approximately the end of April. Completing simple tasks such as getting dressed requires Herculean effort, which exhausts me so much that I have to take those clothes right back off and crawl into bed for the next four, five, or forty-eight hours. Added to my agony is the baffling, crippling pain of fibromyalgia syndrome. Sometimes, between the fatigue, depression, and body aches, the lights begin to flicker in my inner world and I'm sucked into a spiritual black hole that feels utterly void of God's presence. In that unforgiving darkness I grope for him like a blind woman in a strange environment, without her guiding cane.

It's not only darkness I experience in these times, however. Sweet moments of God's presence inexplicably return, like a maddening lover prone to disappearing acts. His wooing leaves me breathless. Then *blam!* That door so full of grace slams shut and it's midnight again, so dark in my soul that my prayers become colorless variations of "Why have you forsaken me?"

In one of those times of impenetrable night I met St. John of the Cross, St. Teresa of Avila's contemporary and friend. His poems, *The Dark Night of the Soul* and *The Spiritual Canticle*, assured me that this man, who lived some 500 years before me, was a kindred spirit. John wrote:

> Where have you hidden,
> Beloved, and left me moaning?
> You fled like the stag
> After wounding me;
> I went out calling, and you were gone.

Not only did John speak to the longing for God so familiar to me, he also addressed the respites of solace that pierced the darkness and filled me with sudden joy. And he did so in language that was infinitely appealing. Rather than sounding lofty and religious, John wrote using exquisitely romantic metaphors that fired my love for my Beloved. This stanza from *The Dark Night of the Soul* hints at the complex relationship between spiritual darkness and the intimacy with God it can shape.

> O you guiding night!
> O night more kindly
> than the dawn!
> O you night that united
> Lover with beloved,
> the beloved in the Lover
> transformed!

Yes! I thought. *I know this night!* and promptly fell in love with the starry-eyed God-lover given to such soaring verse.

You don't have to hang around John long before the sound of Teresa of Avila's laughter steals your attention. I slowly began to look at her published work, too. She emerged from the page immediately as a hoot. The woman was known to tease John mercilessly about his height, which was about the same as a toy action figure. Upon recruiting him and Antonio de Heredia to her cause she quipped to her nuns, "Thanks be to God, daughters! I have found a friar and a half to start the Reform with."

I believe her buoyant personality balanced John's somewhat dour disposition. She reminded him that although joy could be found in the dark night, it's much easier to spot during a walk in the sun.

John showed me how to recline my face on the breast of the Beloved in my bed of affliction, but it was Teresa who charged into my room and flung the drapes open. She assured me that she knew all about being sick and sad, and like her I could overcome all through Christ. In fact, once she had become so ill that her family thought she'd already died and began to prepare her body for burial! There go all my excuses to wallow. No one ever shipped me off to a mortician to be embalmed, although like Teresa I do a remarkable imitation of the dead. I began to trust the funny nun.

Through her prolific writing, Teresa told me about adventures in prayer and God that I hadn't begun to dream of, and what's more, she persuaded me that our good Father God was willing to give *me* these kinds of glorious encounters with him. Her wise words convinced me to take her hand, and she would show me the way to the diamond inside of myself: brilliant, precious, and full of exciting facets to explore.

I had my doubts. She was a nun, and I was married and the mother of a sizable brood. She lived five centuries ago. I was thoroughly postmodern. She was considered a leader of the Counter-Reformation movement. I was born and bred thoroughly Protestant and, despite my love of John of the Cross, had an almost pathological fear of most things Roman Catholic. Teresa led a life of poverty, but I had hundreds of spiritual books, cable television with four different Christian networks, and unlimited wireless Internet access. Yet, I still felt lost most days. How could her centuries-old teachings possibly calm the screeching wilderness within me?

Teresa shushed me. Generally I hate it when people I'm reading shush me, but I suspected she had something important to say. So I quieted myself and continued to read until I came upon her famous bookmark prayer. The words washed over me in waves of peace:

Let nothing upset you,
let nothing startle you.
All things pass;
God does not change.
Patience wins
all it seeks.
Whoever has God
lacks nothing:
God alone is enough.

God alone is *enough*? Now that was a fresh idea for me, a woman who perpetually felt like "enough" was a little more than whatever I had. I found myself not only wanting to *know*—in every way such a concept could be known—that yes indeed, God alone is enough, but I also wanted to know the woman, so unlike myself, who was bold enough in one of the most volatile times in Christian history to say so.

Maybe you, too, are a soul child of the Reformation and never thought you'd show any interest in a saint. Maybe you view *mystical* as yet another word that is best avoided in a Christian vocabulary, or even find the whole idea of mysticism a little silly, but you picked this book up because the idea that God alone is enough speaks to a yearning deep inside of you. Are you willing to put any misgivings you may have aside and give St. Teresa of Avila a chance, if only because she possessed the kind of patience and forbearance to say "Let nothing upset you" and mean it?

If you want to live with such grace-infused assurance, prepare to meet my friend Teresa de Cepeda y Ahumada, a woman responsible for revolutionizing the prayer lives of millions. More important, prepare to meet Christ, Teresa's Beloved, in new, exciting ways. As we travel together, may you find yourself held tightly in his everlasting arms.

Let's pray.

O God,
you taught your beloved Teresa the way of perfection;
nourish us by her delectable teachings.
Set us ablaze, dear one, with desire to know you
as our loving friend.
When our spirits have grown cold,
send us the warmth of the Holy Spirit.
Rekindle the flame of love within us.

Give us soul friends for our pilgrimage,
who will pray with us and share our journey
of learning to enjoy you and give you pleasure.
Set our feet on the path of joy and delight,
and help us to shine with holiness
through Jesus Christ our Lord,
who lives and reigns with you and the Holy Spirit,
one God, now and forever.

Amen.

1

St. Teresa of Avila's Sparkling Life

"My Lord, you seem determined to save me.
I beseech Your Majesty to let it be so."

Whether you're fabulous enough to boast of your own reality television show or so rarely sought after that your mother keeps giving you copies of *How to Win Friends and Influence People*, you're in for a treat. Our guide for this spirited journey enjoyed immense popularity.

The ever-enchanting Teresa of Avila was a stunning beauty. Think dark hair, generous curves, and eyes as black and luminous as obsidian. She was redolent of talent, dancing, singing, and charming her way into the good graces of crowds of admirers who clamored to be near her. As if she didn't have enough unfair advantages, she was a prolific writer, possessing a brilliant theological mind. And God gave her *visions*. Good ones.

THE EARLY YEARS

Teresa wriggled her way into the world in the village of Avila, high amid the mountains of Sierra de Gredos in central Spain. The year was 1515, at the height of the Spanish Inquisition. Although born of noble blood, Teresa's grandfather was a *converso*, a Jew forced to convert to Christianity under threat of torture. At one point he and his sons were made to parade around town dressed in the *sambenitillo con sus cruces*, a knee-length yellow garment marked with black crosses, while bystanders, compelled out of loyalty to the Church, showered them with stones and spittle. For seven consecutive Fridays they donned the humiliating costumes. Teresa's father, Alonso, never forgot the horror of it. The family lived under constant scrutiny after that.

When Teresa writes about her father in her autobiography, she describes him as a principled, scrupulous man. Serious and devout, Don Alonso was a man who, despite the social and racial tensions prevalent in his day, refused to keep slaves. He married Teresa's mother, Beatriz de Ahumada, an extremely beautiful, bright girl, after the death of his first wife. Beatriz could read and write in the Spanish vernacular—although not in Latin, which was the language of schools and the Church. It's likely that it was she who taught Teresa to read and inspired her lifelong love affair with books. It's doubtful Teresa would have been the writer and thinker she became without her mother's influence.

One of thirteen children, Teresa enjoyed the advantages of being a favored child. Her parents doted on her, perhaps because of her gregarious nature, or maybe because from her earliest years Teresa was touched with an inner flame that cast a warm and happy glow on everyone around her.

She learned to read at an early age. Heroic stories of faith and martyrdom deeply affected her. When she wasn't playing hermitage in her orchard, the bossy abbess-to-be made monastics out of all the neighborhood kids. Imagine being her childhood buddy.

"Teresa, wanna play Barbies?"

"Barbies are lame. Let's run away to Africa and preach the gospel to the Moors!"

"But . . . um . . . they'll cut our heads off."

"Yes, but we'll go *straight* to heaven!"

Even if Teresa's station in life allowed her the best toys on the block, I'd dare say no one was interested in the toys alone. She had to be the go-to girl for excitement. In fact, Teresa was so compelling that at a mere seven years old she convinced her little brother Rodrigo to steal away with her on a daring spiritual adventure. They planned to beg their way to the Dark Continent, like the poor friars she'd read about, and in Morocco achieve the glorious martyrdom she dreamed of at the hands of infidels. When Dona Beatriz discovered her children were missing, fraught with anxiety she sent several servants out into the streets to look for the little zealots. Their uncle finally found the pair, not too far from home, and snatched them off the fast track to heaven. He promptly escorted them back to their grateful mother's arms.

Teresa was close to her mother. They devoured books, especially chivalrous tales, which her stern father, who preferred they'd read about the lives of the holy people, disapproved of. "Our reading romance novels bothered my father so much we had to sneak around so he wouldn't catch us." When Teresa was a teen—reports vary, but she was between twelve and fourteen—her cherished mother died during childbirth, leaving her bereft.

"When I began to realize what I had lost, I was overcome with grief. In my misery I threw myself at the feet of an image of our Lady. Weeping, I pleaded with her to be my mother. I have found her to be a kind and merciful ally whenever I've asked for her help. And in the end, she's drawn me to herself."

A girl needs a mother.

Her father tried his best to ease her suffering. He sent for a female cousin to help her manage the choppy waters of bereavement. The girl distracted Teresa with the wholly superficial. They devoured more romance novels until what was once a harmless indulgence became an unruly habit for Teresa. She wasted countless hours hiding from her father, absorbed by the books. "I didn't think I could be happy without a new one." By her own admission, her desire to live a virtuous life grew cold during this time. In her autobiography she wrote: "I longed to please people and began to obsess about how I looked. I had to have the latest fashions, perfumed my skin, and took great care to pamper my hands, and fuss with my hair."

In other words, she became a teenage girl.

She didn't have to work so hard at gilding the proverbial lily. Teresa was quite fetching, and her allure didn't go unnoticed. However, the poor, motherless girl, like many of us, had difficulty grasping exactly how lovable she was.

She knew she was charming; by now she'd become an accomplished flirt. She understood she was "desirable" on many levels, even at such a young age, but that doesn't necessarily satisfy a girl's need to be known and loved for who she authentically is. Poor Teresa. She wanted so badly to live like the heroines she read about, ravished by a devastating lover. Between the books and her neediness she was practically asking for trouble, and eventually she got it.

When Teresa was fifteen or sixteen she fell in love. Using her cousins and maids as accomplices, she smuggled passionate letters to her paramour and swooned over his replies. Accounts of her life during this time give only the sketchiest details, but most scholars agree this was a mild flirtation. That doesn't mean it was without controversy. People in town began to talk, and Don Alonso, still scarred by his childhood experiences of being publicly humiliated, resolved to stave off disaster and protect his daughter's reputation. He promptly shipped Teresa off to a convent that served as a finishing school for well-to-do girls. Augustinian nuns took the lovesick teen in, intent on quenching the fire within her.

Inner fire is difficult to quell, and Teresa's vivaciousness was a brilliant purchaser of favors. Teresa used her gifts of persuasion to convince the unsuspecting nuns to allow her freedoms that other girls at the convent did not enjoy, although she was much more constrained than when she was at home.

But it was also here with the Augustinian nuns that Teresa began to experience deeply satisfying solitude. That and the positive influence of the nuns rekindled her childhood zeal. Her obsession with romantic love began to fade like a conversation she'd lost interest in, and Teresa blessed the Lord for putting up with her foolishness for so long.

As much as she had begun to enjoy her life as a boarder at the convent, she had no desire to be a nun herself. In fact, she was so strongly against the idea that she prayed God would not give her a vocation. She'd formed an amorous attachment to a distant cousin and flirted with the idea of marrying him, but Teresa feared marriage. One source notes, "It is interesting that she later told her nuns how fortunate they were to have avoided [marriage's] drawbacks—which she gave as having to submit totally to a man, and run the risk of an early death through too much childbearing." Surely watching her mother suffer and die in childbirth shaped these ideas.

Toward the end of her time with the Augustinian nuns, Teresa warmed to the idea of being a nun, wondering if perhaps she could do it on her own terms. The willful young woman considered choosing a less austere house. A dear friend was a nun at another convent. She told herself if she ever did take vows—although convinced she wouldn't—maybe she'd join her friend's community.

Her thoughts on the matter weren't altogether frivolous. As Teresa's spiritual life improved she began to debate the question—to be or not to be a nun—so intensely it left her physically ill, and then a series of fortuitous events led Teresa to believe that her sickness was a nudge from God designed to align her with his will. Her sister Maria and her husband sent for her. Halfway between her sister and her father, her virtuous widower uncle Pedro resided. He asked Teresa to visit with him for a short time.

Don Pedro had two favorite topics to talk about: the ways of God and the vanity of the world. When he wasn't waxing eloquently on spiritual truths, he spent much of his time reading inspiring books. He asked Teresa to read to him while she was there. These were no romance novels; the contents sobered Teresa and stirred her to profound introspection. She began to understand that everything is nothing; the world is vanity, and soon enough it will all come to an end. Examining her life she found it wanting and began to fear that if she died she'd go to hell.

She may not have loved the idea of being a nun, but she'd seen some fine examples of godly women at the convent. Teresa reasoned that religious life would probably be the best and safest place for her. Although initially she hated the idea, over a three-month period little by little Teresa forced herself to accept what she'd fought so hard against. She would indeed become a nun, sadly motivated by fear, rather than by love and devotion.

Having made her decision, negative thoughts assailed her, and she wondered if she'd be able to endure the trials of religious life because she'd been so pampered most of her life. Worrying over these matters with such intensity only exacerbated her health problems. High fevers and fainting spells became the norm, which scholars now attribute to malaria. But she had books. Teresa always kept those reliable guides by her side. "My fondness for good books was my salvation. Reading the *Letters of St. Jerome* encouraged me so much I decided to brave telling my father about my decision to put on the habit. I was the kind of person whose word was solid. If I told him I was going to do it, nothing would turn me back."

Don Alonso's reaction was less than enthusiastic; he was adamantly against it! The best she could get out of him was that when he died, she could do whatever she wanted.

The more resistance Teresa encountered, the more her determination swelled. A sense of urgency propelled her now, and she knew she wouldn't be able to wait until her father died. She had to find a creative solution to the challenge her father posed. Being a young woman with powerful natural ambition helped. She'd find a way to stay in the convent, so help her God.

A Vow in the Making

It's ironic that Teresa's one obstacle to becoming a nun was the person who sent her to a convent in the first place. He had wanted her time there to be a teenage version of a "time-out." Teresa was to get a little education, not a lot—too much education for a girl was considered ruinous. Then she would come back home purged and refreshed, and marry well—Don Alonso hoped. And now this! What was a girl desperately seeking sacred vows to do?

Run away, of course. Teresa had more smarts than she had at seven, and she didn't have to drag her little brother Rodrigo along this time. As Clare of Assisi did before her, Teresa eloped with God, defying the wish of her beloved father that she be a nun, literally, over his dead body.

Despite her resolve, leaving him was the most difficult thing she'd ever done. For the most part, her father believed the girl he doted on was incapable of any serious character defect. She knew he'd be shocked by her actions. Because she loved him so, she hated to disobey and disappoint him. But she knew what she must do, and at the age of twenty Teresa entered the Monastery of the Incarnation, even though it caused her tremendous pain.

"When I left my father's house I felt the separation so acutely that I don't think it could have been greater if I were dying. It was as if every bone in my body was being torn apart. My love for God at that time was nothing compared to the love I had for my family. Oh, how my heart constrained me, so that if the Lord had not helped me, I wouldn't have been able to carry on."

Teresa's spiritual elopement did not mean she was a happy bride of Christ. The fact remained: she'd forced herself to enter the convent, motivated by fear of hell and a desire to escape God's displeasure. But her Groom was far more winsome than she believed him to be. A year after she entered the convent, almost immediately after she was clothed in her habit, something shifted inside her.

"The Lord revealed to me how kind he is to those who force themselves to serve him. Within an hour I was so happy with my choice that the feeling never left me, even to this day. Everything about the religious life delighted me. Sometimes, I'd sweep the floor and remember the hours I wasted indulging myself in trivial things like looking good, and I realized I was free from all that now! The joy I experienced amazed me."

Not all nuns were enclosed, or cloistered, in those days. Convents were more like fancy hotels, with vast parlors. They took in affluent girls whose families had no idea what to do with them. The wealthy maidens brought their servants, jewels, and lap dogs with them. Because food was scarce at the convents, scads of visitors were encouraged to join them on the weekends, bearing gifts.

The Monastery of the Incarnation enjoyed this kind of mitigated rule and teemed with social activity. Teresa, with her keen intellect and talents combined with her startling good looks, quickly became a parlor favorite.

Men visited regularly. These devotees would come ostensibly for spiritual guidance, but they found Teresa irresistible. The motherless woman-child bloomed before their admiration. She responded to their favor by falling in love with one after another of them.

Teresa pined for visiting days when she could revel in enrapturing her admirers. But as much as she craved being the center of attention, she began to feel guilty about all the time she spent engaged in social discourse. Guilt prodded reflection, and Teresa turned a critical eye on herself.

She did not like what she saw. Because she was an extremist by nature, Teresa began to accuse herself mercilessly, which did nothing for her health. Her fainting spells caused by the malaria increased, joined now by mysterious and severe chest pains. Doctors also diagnosed her with tuberculosis and severe nerve damage, although they seemed powerless to help her. Teresa wrote in her autobiography that she had many other illnesses, which could have included epilepsy. In any case, her first year in the convent was consumed by poor health.

Teresa's father sought relief for her. In his desperation he took her to a nearby *curandera*, a well known folk healer.

On her way to see the woman, Teresa received from her uncle a book by Francisco de Osuna called *The Third Spiritual Alphabet*. It taught a method of mental prayer that intrigued Teresa, called recollection. "I didn't know how to proceed in prayer, and so I was very happy with this book, and determined to follow that path with all my strength."

The premise of the Franciscan mystic's book was that friendship and communion with God are possible by entering your heart, resting in loving stillness, and finally rising above even the heart to God alone. You might know this kind of prayer by another name, "contemplative prayer." For nine months *The*

Third Spiritual Alphabet was Teresa's constant companion, but she had no one to teach her beyond its pages. Her progress was minimal, but God began to grant her lovely gifts as she toddled along on this path.

Sometimes God surprised her with a peace-infused sense of quiet, unlike anything she'd ever experienced. Other times, she'd feel a spectacular melding with him, and she would free-fall into his arms so completely that her soul would become utterly absorbed. In this happy union with God all her concerns would vanish, even though her body remained sick.

The *curandera* only made matters worse. In truth the woman was the sixteenth-century equivalent of a quack. Her harsh regime of purgatives, emetics, and herbal remedies were harder on Teresa's body than her illnesses were, but Teresa remained with the woman for almost a year. While there, Teresa became convinced that her illness was of a spiritual nature and sought out a confessor to aid her in finding her sick soul's cure.

There was just one problem: the only priest in town was burdened by a weakness for the fairer sex. As it was, the young priest had spent seven years involved in an affair with a bewitching local woman. Literally, the woman bewitched him with a copper amulet that she made him promise to wear as a token of their love. This priest to whom Teresa spent so much time confessing her sins turned and confessed *his* to *her*. Bright Teresa identified the amulet as a primary source of his woes, and at her urging the smitten priest banished the object from his person. Then, he wasted not a moment transferring his immense love to Teresa.

Teresa returned his affection, but not seriously. She was more in love with God and credits the first inklings of devotion she'd gained in prayer as keeping her out of harm's way. She insisted the priest keep his mind on heavenly things instead of earthly pleasures, something she admitted she would have found hard to do in another, less prayer-full time in her life. Our Teresa was growing up.

Since the besotted priest failed to give her proper spiritual direction, she didn't find any relief from her suffering, even spiritually. To make matters worse, the *curandera*'s dubious methods almost killed her. Teresa's fevers soared, and nausea prevented her from eating. Ravaged by disease, she began to waste away. And how her body hurt. Fiery nerve pain shot through her body, causing unbearable pain. Her father brought her home to die.

For three or four months Teresa languished. Her beloved books helped; reading focused her attention and drew her back to the peace-infused quiet and extraordinary sense of union with God she'd previously experienced, but near the end of this time, a coma dimmed her bright light. She became so gravely ill that her breath and heartbeat diminished until they were undetectable. Her family dug her grave.

"They administered the sacrament of the anointing of the sick, and from hour to hour and moment to moment, they expected me to die. Again and again they recited the Creed to me. As if I could understand them! At one point they were so sure I was dead, they waxed my eyelids shut."

She may not have been dead, but she was in a terrible state. "I had bitten my tongue to pieces. I was so weak my throat could not so much as swallow water. All my bones seemed out of joint, and my head was a jumble of confusion. I'd curled up like a ball, no more able to move my arms, feet, hands, or head than a corpse. I think I could manage to flick a single finger on my right hand. That was it." But Teresa insisted on returning to the convent, where she remained gravely ill for eight months and partially paralyzed for the next three years. When she could finally crawl on her hands and knees, Teresa praised God for his goodness.

"I suffered those years with gladness," she said, taking no credit for her tranquility. "If that patience hadn't come from the hand of His Majesty, it would have been impossible to suffer so much with so great contentment."

MEETING THE BELOVED

When her health was restored, life in the convent continued much as it did the first time. Teresa the social butterfly returned to the parlor and flitted about from visitor to visitor on the wings of the attention they lavished on her. And just as she had before, she berated herself about her intense need for praise. She hadn't yet grown the courage to follow God without the luxurious feelings of acceptance she'd come to depend on from the parlor people. It seems the death of her mother had left a cavernous hole in her soul, rendering her powerless to avoid the place where she felt such an outpouring of affection, even if her reliance on the attention—her craving for it—ultimately hurt her. In her mind she was like the greatest of deceivers: outwardly devout, and inwardly in shambles. She became disgusted with herself, until even her semblance of piety slipped. More and more she engaged in petty sins. The joy she felt in doing good faded, and her taste for virtue waned.

"This was the worst trick the devil could play on me. Seeing myself as wicked, I was afraid to pray. A host of vanities spoiled me, and I was ashamed to return to God in the special friendship I'd found with him through prayer."

It was easier for her to simply recite the obligatory rote prayers she learned at the convent than to enjoy the intimate experience of prayer she'd stumbled upon in reading *The Third Spiritual Alphabet*. She blamed her illness for her spiritual inertia and let a whole year lapse without praying in the way that had become so meaningful to her. Only a short time later, Teresa would suffer another devastating blow. Her father became ill with what was most likely bone cancer. She left the convent to care for him but found his dying excruciating. She reflected:

"I loved that man so much that as I saw his death approaching, I felt like my soul was being torn from my body."

Having your soul ripped out has to hurt like the dickens, and Teresa had already suffered the thorny pain of losing her mother. This was too much for her to bear. She began to shut down her fragile emotions and returned to the convent after her father's death feeling about as solid as gas. She remained that way, cut off from feeling, an airy, chatty, worldly nun, until some twenty years later—when a statue, of all things, rocked her world.

It was an ordinary day, although busy. The not quite forty-year-old prioress was engrossed in getting the convent ready for a festival. Another monastery had loaned the sisters a statue. It had arrived in one piece—thankfully—and Teresa, entering the oratory, stumbled upon the image of the Suffering Christ, the *Ecce Homo*. This was no placid work of art. It was a gut-punching, graphic, deeply disturbing representation of a brutalized Christ, with three-dimensional, torn, and bloody wounds. Think Mel Gibson's *The Passion of the Christ*, in a single statue.

"The sight of it utterly destroyed me, wrenching the deepest devotion from me. I felt keenly, painfully aware of what Christ had suffered for us, and how little thankfulness I offered him in return. I threw myself at his feet, my heart broken, and begged him to give me the strength, once and for all, to never forsake him again.

"I had no more trust in myself, and placed every ounce of faith I had in God. I think I told him right then that I would stay there, wrapped around his feet, weeping profusely, until he gave me what I wanted."

She suddenly realized: she wanted so much more of *him*.

Teresa indeed stayed there, baptized in tears of penance, letting the waters of her contrition begin to transform her into a woman who would come to know Christ so intimately she'd call him her Beloved. The wounded Christ, savagely scourged, had touched her to her core in a way the Christ of her past, whom she perceived as constantly judging her, had not. The way she prayed began to change again. "Since I couldn't seem to make reflections with my intellectual understanding, I visualized Christ within me."

Now in her innermost being she would look for his face, bloodied by a crown of thorns. She felt best when she meditated on the mysteries of his life when he was most lonely, and she came to a profound conclusion: "It seemed to me that when he was alone and afflicted, like someone in a lot of trouble, Christ would need me. He *had* to accept me."

Teresa imagined herself being a friend of Jesus as he prayed in the garden. If she could, she'd think of his blood-stained sweat and his agony in knowing he'd be the Passover lamb for the whole world. "I desired to wipe his brow, but I never did. I was too sinful, but I stayed with him as long as my thoughts allowed me to."

For years to come she would ponder those images before she fell asleep at night. She didn't exactly know what she was doing, but the practice became as habitual to her as making the sign of the cross.

Although she was progressing, she lacked fellow pilgrims to travel with who understood her. She was given a copy of St. Augustine's *Confessions*. Teresa was already fond of his writings, but now she identified with the famous former sinner. Like her, Augustine had a keen intellect and considerable appetite for that which was not so good for his soul. "As I begin to read the

Confessions, I found my own story there. When I came upon the passage about how he heard the child's voice in the garden saying, 'Take and read,' and was in that moment converted, I felt in my heart that the Lord was calling *me*. Overcome by emotion, I dissolved into weary tears."

Not only was God reaffirming the message that he *desired* Teresa, and not in the way that men or even other people who enjoyed her attention had, he was teaching her that he gives grace. For all her poverty of spirit, God was passing out spiritual riches. He expected the moments of intimacy he lavishly bestowed upon her to be received with joy rather than guilt. To deny them would be false humility.

"One day while I was in prayer, the Lord wanted to show me only his hands, which were so incredibly beautiful I could never begin to describe them!" The vision frightened her, as all these new experiences of intimacy with Christ did initially, but she knew the vision was authentic. A few days later he showed her his divine face. It left her completely consumed.

And sometime later, "he granted me the favor of seeing his entire self! I couldn't understand why he showed me himself, little by little. I realized later that he'd given me all I could handle at one time. So much glory all at once would have been unbearable to one as lowly and wretched as I."

Jesus appeared—no pun intended—to love Teresa very much. Their divine/human romance was so riveting, so irresistible, that her most famous vision—the wounding of her heart—became the inspired subject of Italian sculptor Gian Lorenzo Bernini:

Exhibit A: The words of Teresa:

"Sometimes love, like an arrow, is thrust into the deepest part of the heart and the soul doesn't know what has happened or what it wants, except all it wants is God. The soul feels as if the arrow has been dipped in a poisonous herb that makes it despise itself for love of him. This pierced soul would gladly lose its life for him. You can't explain this. It's impossible to exaggerate the way God wounds the soul, or the agony this causes, for the soul forgets itself. Yet this pain is so exquisite—so delightful—that no other pleasure in life gives greater happiness.

"Oh, how many times in this state do I remember the words of David: 'As the deer longs for streams of water, so my soul longs for you, O God.' I experience it literally when he wounds me.

"Sometimes in this state I saw a vision: an angel in bodily form, standing very close to me on my left side. The angel was not large, but small and very beautiful. His face was so aflame that I thought he must be a cherub, one of the highest order of angels, who seem to be made of fire.

"I saw that his hands held a great golden dart, and at the end of the iron tip fire plumed. The angel plunged the flaming dart through my heart again and again until it penetrated my innermost core. When he withdrew it, it felt like he was carrying the deepest part of me away with him. He left me on fire, consumed with the immense love of God. The pain was so fierce that it made me moan, and its sweetness so utterly divine it abolished any desire to take it away; nor is the soul content with anything but God.

This is what Bernini sculpted Teresa's encounter to look like:

I'll have what she's having.

LATER GRACES

While the voices and visions Teresa experienced were powerful, she still wrestled with them. "At that time the devil was preying on certain women who had fallen into serious delusions. I was terrified that I too would be deceived, not that I could avoid the wonderful delight and sweetness I had been experiencing. Besides, in the end I always felt the greatest assurance that these gifts came from God, especially when I received them in prayer."

Her trust was not in herself, for Teresa was ruthless in examining her flaws. Many times in reading her work I wondered if she shouldn't have had a talk with the sixteenth-century version of Dr. Phil. Then again, in those days he may have been inclined to agree with her grim assessments.

It was jarring to my postmodern mind to find such a powerful woman so unrelentingly self-deprecating. *Girlfriend, you need some self-esteem*, I thought, again and again. However, as I continued journeying with her, I realized that she was a product of her time. Women had few opportunities and were considered inferior to men. She also composed her works under duress, while the Inquisition raged on. Teresa was wily enough to speak the truth but downplayed herself so completely it would have been hard for anyone to think of her as a haughty woman, wanting to usurp authority they didn't believe she had.

Second, I believe she was so hard on herself for a more important reason: Christ had showed himself to her. The prophet Isaiah had a similar experience:

In the year that King Uzziah died, I saw the Master sitting on a throne—high, exalted!—and the train of his robes filled the Temple. Angel-seraphs hovered above him, each with six wings. With two wings they covered their faces, with two their feet, and with two they flew. And they called back and forth one to the other, "Holy, Holy, Holy is God-of-the-Angel-Armies. His bright glory fills the whole earth."

The foundations trembled at the sound of the angel voices, and then the whole house filled with smoke. I said, "Doom! It's Doomsday! I'm as good as dead! Every word I've ever spoken is tainted—blasphemous even! And the people I live with talk the same way, using words that corrupt and desecrate. And here I've looked God in the face!" (Isaiah 6:1–8)

Looking God in the face changes everything. How could a person be dishonest about their ugliness before such awesome beauty?

Teresa began to rigorously examine her visions and subject them to a host of spiritual directors for scrutiny as well. Often the men who offered her guidance mistrusted her or simply gave her wretched advice. One spiritual director saw her potential and treated her as though she were a spiritual giant.

"He started out determined to guide me, as if I were a remarkably strong person. By all rights I should have been, considering what I'd told him about my experiences in prayer. He didn't want me to offend God, but when I saw he was intent on having me give up all these little things I had no fortitude to release so perfectly and immediately, I was distressed. He wanted me to die to my soul's attachments all at once. I realized I'd have to be very careful in my relationship with him."

Be careful in her relationship with him? That was a gutsy attitude for a woman of her time.

She wrote, "What I'm trying to say is that, though well-meaning, his suggestions would not have helped me. They were suited to a more perfected soul. As for me, I may have been advanced in terms of the favors I had received from God, but I was a beginner when it came to virtue."

Unfortunately, being misunderstood and misdirected would plague Teresa most of her life. As she grew in power and influence she disturbed religious and political leaders, many of whom were jealous of her. Teresa was repeatedly reported to the Inquisition, which ruthlessly inspected her. Writing was dangerous for a nun—for a *woman*. During this time she could have easily achieved the martyrdom she had craved as a child. Every risky word she put down is worthy of our attention for that reason alone, but one has only to dive into her work to experience the wonderland of her clever mind. Sure, she rambled a bit, but she wrote fast and never had the time or inclination to self-edit. Under such circumstances can you blame her?

Beginning in 1562, when Teresa was forty-seven, she founded seventeen monasteries. Five years later she met John of the Cross, her dear friend and confessor. They urged one another to deeper depths of being in love with Love himself and experienced divine favors together. Once, a nun entering the kitchen to turn the coals came upon the pair chatting. They'd stayed up all night steeped in God talk and God love. The nun reported that they were inclined toward each other, their heads close together, oblivious to the outside world. Both their chairs appeared to be hovering inches above the floor. Now that's *high talk!*

Amid wrathful persecution, petty jealousies, and increasing ill health, Teresa continued to work, traveling extensively. No luxurious jet planes whisked her to her destinations. She traveled by donkey and a rickety carriage in appalling, dangerous conditions to the medieval versions of fleabag motels. *Not* good!

Teresa suffered tremendously, but she never lost touch with her Beloved. She was a genius administrator and spiritual guide, but the sassy nun was humble enough to do kitchen duty. She was fond of saying how easily she found God amid the pots and pans. In fact, Teresa found her Beloved everywhere; his unceasing sweet talk ever sounded in her ears.

Yet Teresa lived a fully integrated life with love at the heart of her exhaustive work. She was both Mary and Martha in spirit, knowing, "Martha and Mary must share in showing hospitality to Jesus if he were to stay present. They'd be poor hosts if they failed to give him something to eat. How could Mary provide him food if she were always sitting at his feet?"

She lived her life with glorious attention, and while she lived in God's presence she kept her feet (mostly) planted on earth. In one of the most delightful stories about her, Teresa was devouring partridge during a meal. She tore into the bird with gusto. When her behavior shocked her fellow diners she remarked, "When I fast I fast; when I eat partridge, I eat partridge."

Despite her verve, Teresa led a rigorous life. Although she began her existence indulged as a favorite child, her once soft hands calloused from the grueling work she did. But God, who once showed her his own hands, found her altogether lovely. He rewarded her tireless efforts with more of his sweetness, drawing her deeper within the chamber where his most valuable riches lay.

"By taking this road we gain such precious treasures that it is no wonder that the cost is so high," Teresa said. "Eventually we will realize that everything we have paid has been like nothing at all in comparison with the prize's greatness."

Teresa paid a high price indeed, but she saw it all as opportunities to be with Christ. She prayed, "If there is any way I can imitate you I will suffer all trials that come my way and count them as a great blessing. Lord, let us go together; wherever you go, I must go, and I must pass through whatever you must pass."

She meant that to the death. In her poem *Aspirations toward Eternal Life*, she wrote:

> Only with that surety
> I will die do I live,
> Because in dying
> My hope in living is assured.
> Death, bringing life,
> Do not tarry; I await you.

Death did not tarry long at all.

The Longed-for Hour

The fall of 1582 was particularly hard on Teresa. She'd begun to hemorrhage from what many believe now was uterine cancer. It was at this time that she was asked to travel in what, by modern standards, were horrid conditions, at the behest of a duchess who insisted Teresa attend the birth of her first grandchild. She wanted a high and holy person to attend to her daughter-in-law, an absurd and selfish request. Teresa's poor health made the trip more difficult than usual, and she arrived just after the baby came into the world.

"God be praised," Teresa said, good-humored despite being bone weary. "They won't need the saint."

Relieved from her duty to the duchess, she took to bed immediately and would never rise—in this life—again. She was utterly Teresa however, even in the end. Ever penitential, she repeated a psalm of contrition and repentance on her deathbed. She remained self-deprecating. "Don't imitate the poor example this bad nun has set. Forgive me."

When a priest brought her the Blessed Sacrament, she struggled to prostrate herself, crying, "My Lord, and my Bridegroom. The longed-for hour has come. Now it's time for us to meet, my Beloved."

After she'd received Holy Communion, she repeated again and again, "I am a daughter of the Church," perhaps with more than a little irony. For at times Teresa confounded the Roman Catholic Church. Sometimes she distressed Church leaders, but ultimately Teresa reformed many of the sons and daughters who would lead churches and religious institutions into the future. Her reach is astonishing. St. Teresa of Avila is still reforming Christians today, turning them into followers of Christ, not just in name, but in experience. And not just nuns, but the many people who discover her anew each year. She accomplishes this by pointing us to a way of praying that is intimate, important, consuming, and brings the soul into union with God.

Teresa went to sleep in the arms of her Beloved on October 4, 1582. Her death is the stuff of legends. It is said that for days before she passed away, the sweet aroma of lilies filled her room. One story claims that at the moment she died a white dove flew from under her bedcovers—or maybe some wise soul created that fanciful tale as a metaphor to express how her soul took flight, at long last. Another account says that a tree outside her window, which had shed its leaves, exploded into bloom. Whatever the truth may be, what we know is that Teresa's life and teachings were like a seed, which fell into the soil to die. After her death her teachings took root, grew strong, and bloomed, filling Spain, all of Europe, and now the whole world with its sweetness.

St. Teresa of Avila was what we postmodern pilgrims would call *all that*: beautiful, vivacious, a great dancer, excellent cook, skilled horsewoman, and formidable chess player. She was a humble brainiac, wisecracking warrior, impossible dreamer, and spiritual mother. Once, on her travels to attend to yet another vital service, her carriage got stuck in the mud. Teresa called out to God, "If this is how you treat your friends, it's no wonder you have so few of them!" If he didn't have many, Teresa made it her business to be a good one. She was more than his friend; she was God's *sweetheart*! I think we can rely on her to lead us somewhere beautifully beyond yet inside ourselves.

2

Exactly Where Are We Going?

"We do not need wings to search for him.
We need only to find a place where we can be alone
and look upon him present within us."

I subtitled this book "A Spirited Journey with St. Teresa of Avila" for a reason. We're actually going somewhere; we're setting off to visit God's home, and I want it to be fun. Many people think of God's home as being heaven. Certainly Teresa did as a child, which is the main reason why she stole away with her little brother seeking to become a seven-year-old martyr. Fortunately, we don't have to die on this pilgrimage to get to our destination. Well, in a way we do, but let's not get into anything spooky right now. Suffice it to say that where we're going—God's home—exists inside of us.

But how will we go within?

Prayer is going to take us there, just as it did our spirited guide, Teresa. So consider this a prayer pilgrimage. We're going to look at Teresa's major teachings on prayer, and then do some of the very same things she did. Because we have the benefit of her experience, we won't have to flounder as much as she did. Oh, we'll stumble a bit, I'm sure, and that's okay. We don't have to be experts for this trip. All we have to do is prepare to deepen a friendship we already have.

I don't mean with Teresa, though rest assured we will get to know her better also. Mostly we're going to do what those whimsical disciples in the musical *Godspell* urged us to do: see the Lord more clearly, love him more dearly, and follow him more nearly, day by day.

Deepening a friendship sounds straightforward enough, but people have a way of complicating prayer. Even Jesus' disciples, who had the benefit of walking alongside him, were befuddled at how to approach God. "Lord, teach us to pray!" they cried, and many of his followers today are asking him the same thing.

I like the way Eugene Peterson paraphrases Jesus' answer to his disciples in Matthew 6:1–13:

> "Be especially careful when you are trying to be good so that you don't make a performance out of it. It might be good theater, but the God who made you won't be applauding. . . . And when you come before God, don't turn that into a theatrical production either. All these people

making a regular show out of their prayers, hoping for stardom! Do you think God sits in a box seat?

"Here's what I want you to do: Find a quiet, secluded place so you won't be tempted to role-play before God. Just be there as simply and honestly as you can manage. The focus will shift from you to God, and you will begin to sense his grace."

Just be there? Simply and honestly? Jesus sure makes it easy on us, doesn't he?

"The world is full of so-called prayer warriors who are prayer-ignorant. They're full of formulas and programs and advice, peddling techniques for getting what you want from God. Don't fall for that nonsense."

You mean prayer isn't complicated? I don't have to have stacks of books, go to expensive conferences, or master esoteric techniques?

"This is your Father you are dealing with, and he knows better than you what you need. With a God like this loving you, you can pray very simply. Like this:

"Our Father in heaven,
Reveal who you are.
Set the world right;

Do what's best—as above, so below.

Keep us alive with three square meals.

Keep us forgiven with you and forgiving others.

Keep us safe from ourselves and the Devil.

You're in charge!

You can do anything you want!

You're ablaze in beauty!

Yes. Yes. Yes."

Yes, yes, yes, indeed!

"Wait a minute, girl!" you may say. "That's not the Lord's Prayer I know."

I like to shake things up a bit. Many people pray the Our Father that sounds like this:

Our Father which art in heaven, hallowed be thy name.

Thy kingdom come, thy will be done on earth, as it is
   in heaven.

Give us this day our daily bread.

And forgive us our trespasses, as we forgive those who
   trespass against us.

And lead us not into temptation, but deliver us from evil:

For thine is the kingdom, and the power, and the glory,
   forever, and ever.

Amen.

Be honest. Did you rush through reading that because it's so familiar? I won't judge you if you did. At my parish we sing the Lord's Prayer. St. Augustine said, "He who sings prays twice." I feel doubly blessed each and every time I belt out the words, hands clasped with my fellow parishioners, our arms raised toward heaven, while the music lifts our hearts to the Lord. But if I'm honest I'll have to admit, in my private devotions I've muddled through saying it far too many times.

For many of us the Lord's Prayer is an exercise in rote recitation, prattled so thoughtlessly it's lost all meaning. It wasn't much better in Teresa's day.

She says, "When I repeat the 'Our Father,' I think it should be a matter of love for me to understand who this Father is. It will be well too, for us to see who the master is who teaches us this prayer."

It should be matter of *love*? Uh-oh. How many of us actually think about the Our Father this way, each and every time we pray it? I'd venture to say not as many as there should be. A more important question is, how do we go from mindlessly uttering the words to not only being mindful of what we're saying, and whom we're saying it to, but to falling in love with our *Father*? And what about the second part of Teresa's startling statement? How do we begin to see the master who teaches us this prayer?

Stay tuned!

● ● ●

It may be helpful to begin with a before and after view of Teresa's prayer life.

Before: When Teresa arrived as a young nun at the Monastery of the Incarnation, she learned formal, vocal prayers and also tried out a few arbitrary meditation techniques popular at the time. Despite this training, by her own admission she had no idea how to proceed in prayer, or how to recollect herself. All that changed when her uncle gave her Francisco de Osuna's *The Third Spiritual Alphabet.*

I love that he named his book *The Third Spiritual Alphabet.* It reminds me of those Little Golden Books I grew up with. You know them: *The Poky Little Puppy,* or *The Saggy Baggy Elephant.* Reading that title, you can't help but think he's going to offer a way of praying that's *doable.* And that's exactly how Osuna intended his work to be viewed. The humble man believed Jesus meant what he said when he told us to become as children. He organized his work according to the letters of the alphabet, and *The Third Spiritual Alphabet* was part of his ABCs of recollection series.

Did you notice that word, *recollection*? Teresa uses it frequently in her writing. What exactly does it mean? And what does it have to do with prayer?

When I first saw the word I kept tripping over it, thinking it meant "to remember," but Teresa explains it this way. "It is called recollection because the soul collects all the faculties together and enters within itself to be with its God."

You could simplify the concept even more, stripping it down to its most basic function, at least for our purposes: recollection is prayer. It requires attention, even though we postmoderns are driven to unprecedented degrees of distraction. But Osuna admonishes us to discipline our souls gently, and with love. He believed recollection was not achieved by force, but with skill. He said, "Nothing is more skillful than love." This humble man even used a toy as an example: he thought love should be used "like the whip used to start a top so it will spin again and always turn without falling over." Then off you go with God!

I have my own toy metaphor. Imagine you're a child who has, in the course of a day, scattered your toys all around your room. Now imagine a tender, benevolent parent urging you to tidiness. With that sweet, comforting voice guiding you, going from toy to toy, gathering your things, and putting them away isn't so difficult.

At first, you may resist the work of bringing your scattered toys to the toy chest. After all, you're only four years old. You're unfocused. You may still want to play with that stuff, but the voice of the kind parent compels. You are not beaten, berated, or abused. You have a good parent, and for that reason you're compelled to obey (at least some part of you is).

Love is the parent. It compels you with gentleness and grace. The gathering you're doing is recollection. Your toys are those faculties I mentioned, which include your thoughts, intellect, imagination, and memories. One by one you're gently taking them to the toy box. Only it isn't really a toy box you're going to at all. It's more like a treasure chest full of infinite riches.

Here's where the metaphor becomes like a dream, and you get to be more than one character: you yourself can also be the parent, using your will to gather your thoughts. There's more fun. You're also the treasure chest, for you are tenderly directing your thoughts within. Inside of you, your great treasure, God's indwelling presence, is waiting.

For nine months Teresa kept *The Third Spiritual Alphabet* close by. She spent more time in solitude and went to confession often. Although the book said she should be beyond missing the mark, she still struggled with petty sins. But God rewarded her consistency despite herself. Brief, God-infused moments of quiet and a sense of union with the divine began visiting her more often, although she didn't understand them.

This is what her prayer life looked like: "I tried as hard as I could to keep Jesus Christ, our God and our Lord, present with me. That's how I prayed. I would reflect on one of the mysteries of the Lord's life, and try to see the scene represented within me. But most of my time was spent reading good books."

Why such a simple approach? Mostly because Teresa believed she was a failure in prayer, as did youth ministry specialist and spiritual writer Mike Yaconelli. He wrote a poem about it called "A Terrible Prayer." This excerpt speaks for multitudes of us:

I have always been terrible at praying.
I forget.
My mind wanders.
I fall asleep.

I don't pray enough.
I don't understand what prayer is
or what prayer does.
If prayer were a school . . .
I would flunk praying.

Being a prayer failure has its benefits, however. People who pray well are especially apt to defend themselves against distraction and sin. Not us prayer failures. We're a lot more in touch with our poverty of spirit. We attention-deficit types know we need help, and so, like Teresa, we're inclined to throw ourselves on the resources of others. This is why books were so important to our guide. At one time in her life, except for after Communion, Teresa didn't dare begin to pray without a book. "Books were my companions. They shielded me from the blows of many distracting thoughts. They comforted me. Without a book my soul felt dry and my thoughts wandered. With one, I could collect my thoughts. They were the bait that lured my mind back to awareness of God."

The Lord had abundant mercy on Teresa, even as she made her first, fledgling attempts to pray. He will have mercy on us, too. It's okay if, just like Jesus' disciples, we beg on a regular basis, "Lord, teach us to pray," and it's fine if, like Teresa, we have no idea how to proceed in prayer or to recollect ourselves. That's why we're here.

Shall we begin our journey within? It won't be easy, but it'll be *good*. All you need to take with you is a willingness to pray and a desire to fall in love with God. A little humility wouldn't hurt either.

Every pilgrimage has rest stops, so at the end of most of the chapters we're going to pause, reflect, and sometimes pray. You don't have to linger long during these intervals, but I do encourage you to at least enjoy a brief repose. Our pilgrimage won't yield as many benefits if you don't actively participate.

I'm so excited! The Beloved is already waiting for us, just like the father in the biblical story of the prodigal son. When God sees us walking toward him, he will run—not walk—to meet us and cover our face with kisses.

Teresa knew that for some of us, taking the first few steps is the hardest part of the journey. Maybe you're the kind of starter who feels like you have to wait until everything, including you, is perfect: you're sinless, placid as a lake, and have a comfortable, quiet, pastoral environment to pray in.

Nice life if you can get it, but you can't get it. None of us have that kind of perfection to work with. We're going to begin like Charlotte Elliot's hymn says, just as we are without one plea. And we're going to begin right now. Wherever you are, take a few moments to offer yourself to God. You can do this silently, or say something simple like, "God, I'm yours." You can even pray one of my favorite prayers: "Lord, have mercy on me."

Next, review Teresa's words below. I've jotted them down as if they were poetry. Everyone knows you have to pay closer attention to poetry. Consider how the Psalms use the word *selah* to urge you to stop and listen. Add your own *selah*s as you read, and stop to hear what Teresa is saying to your soul. When you have listened with your heart, give thanks.

• • •

St. Teresa's Advice for Beginners and Failures in Prayer

The Lord told me:

"Get started as best as you can.

You will see what I can do."

Oh, my friends,

How well have I seen it!

How you begin is all-important.

Only with resolute determination,

Will you persevere to the end of the journey.

Come what may,

Happen what may.

Whatever work is involved,

Whatever criticism arises.

Whether you arrive,

Or die on the road.

With courage,

Or without it,

Even if the whole world

Collapses . . .

Pray.

His Majesty is the friend of courageous souls

Who walk in humility without trusting in themselves.

Cowardly souls, and those who feign humility

Crawl along the bottom of this path.
It takes years for them to advance
As far as the courageous do
In only a few.
Be courageous.
Strive for great things along the path.

The greatest labor is in the beginning.
It is the beginner who works
But the Lord gives the increase.
In the other degrees of prayer
The greatest thing is
Enjoying.
Whether in the beginning,
The middle, or the end,
All bear their different crosses.
If you don't want to get lost,
Walk along the path Christ trod.
Blessed be the trials
so superabundantly repaid
even here in this life.

The world is full of simple treats

PURE POETRY

PASSIONS

3

Make a Garden

"The beginner must see himself as making a garden for the delight of his Beloved."

We have already seen the major milestones of Teresa's life. Now, we'll explore her autobiography in a completely different way, for nestled within its pages is one of the most sublime analogies about prayer ever written.

Oh sure, while she teaches she lambasts her abilities so often that you may feel an urge to shout, "Get a grip. You're not a worm!" But I assure you it will pass as her wit and astute insights distract you from what sounds suspiciously like self-loathing. So many treasures lie within her autobiography, and we are going to find them.

Like Jesus, Teresa took the most ordinary things and spun them into startling parables. Here she likens the soul to a garden, beginning in her standard, self-deprecating way, "It seems to me I read or heard this metaphor somewhere." Picture her waving her hands as she speaks: "My memory is so poor, I have no idea where it came from, but it'll work for my purposes now. The beginner must see himself as making a garden for the delight of his Beloved. But the soil is very barren and full of noxious weeds. His Majesty himself pulls up the weeds and replaces them with good seed. Keep in mind that all this is done before you even set out to learn how to pray."

Already we're ahead! The mere fact that we've begun this pilgrimage is the greatest indicator that God is working in us. I don't know about you, but many times I've thought my garden was only poison ivy and oak gone wild. It was scary enough for me to think about going in. I wouldn't dare invite the Beloved inside. I thought he'd only be repelled, but how I longed for his help to manage my dry, craggy, weed-filled soil. I'd have settled for having his presence while I battered the ground that was my wicked heart. I felt forsaken too much of the time. I was so misguided.

Oh, to have known in those times that my kind Beloved had no fear of what he'd find when he visited me. He wasn't standing above me, grim-faced and judgmental, as I endlessly toiled, getting sunburned and erupting in skin rashes. Not that I made real progress. Most of the time I was clueless as to what would make my garden grow. But he was there all the time, before I arrived, before I even realized I had a garden. He was right there, hunkered down, doing the hard work of making my soul his resting place. As much as I like the thought of donning a pair of brand-new floral garden gloves and kicking my feet into those cute rubber clogs, garden tools in hand, I don't need any of those things to begin the work we're about to do, because preparing soil and pulling weeds is God's business.

This is a pretty radical idea. Imagine what it sounded like in the sixteenth century, during the Inquisition! But I believe Teresa assured us that we mustn't get caught up in worrying about our vices because we aren't meant to do what God does best. We have our own jobs.

All good gardeners must labor. God's done the difficult prep work, braving the noxious, unwelcoming weeds, but we have our own task. Our job is to take the time to water the plants he's started so they don't die. We want our plants to take root, shoot from the soil, bud, and flower. Soon they'll grow lush enough to perfume the whole garden with their fragrances. Our Beloved will find this so refreshing that he'll come to our gardens often, finding his joy amid our sweet-smelling virtues. But how do we get there from here?

Teresa gives us the broad picture:

> Now let's see how we need to water the garden, so we'll understand what we have to do, how much the labor will cost us, if the time and work we put into it is worth it, and how long it will last. Our garden can be watered in four ways: We can draw water from a well, which is a lot of work. Or you can get the water by turning the crank of a waterwheel and

drawing it through an aqueduct. I've tried this myself and know it's not as much trouble to do as the first way. And you get more water.

Or you can channel the water from the flow of a river or stream. The garden is watered much better this way because the ground is saturated and you don't have to water it as frequently. This is a lot less work for the gardener.

Or the water may come from an abundant rain pouring on the soil; the Lord waters the garden himself, without any work on our part. This is by far the best method of all.

So, if the garden is the soul, and we are the gardeners—in cooperation with God—what exactly is this water? I'll let Teresa answer. "The four ways of watering the garden in order to maintain it are the four degrees of prayer that the Lord in his goodness has sometimes placed in my soul. Without water everything will die."

It's all quite simple: our garden needs water. Teresa says, "Nothing I've found is more appropriate to explain spiritual experiences. . . . I'm so fond of this element I've observed it more than any other." She spoke of three relevant properties that water has: If you're hot, it will cool you off. "It'll even cool off large fires." I'm sure I don't have to tell you "hot" and "fire" have multiple implications here, which I'll leave to your imagination. The second property of water is its ability to clean dirty things. Teresa asks, "Do you know what cleansing properties there are in this living water, this heavenly water, this clear water when it is unclouded, free from mud, and comes down from heaven? Once the soul has drunk of this water, it purifies and cleanses it from all sins."

And Teresa explains a third property of water: it quenches thirst. "Thirst means the desire for something so necessary that if we do not have it we will die." And to Teresa, prayer satisfies the most insatiable thirsts. It can also show us our spiritual blind spots. Hold a glass of water up. It looks clear, but if you hold it up to the light, you can see the dust particles. In prayer, God can reveal our weaknesses.

You may have noticed I haven't given you an itemized list of what the four degrees of prayer are, complete with bullets and explanations. I thought about it. I even tried, and I ended up confused. The challenge is that the degrees aren't as precise as Teresa made them sound in her lovely metaphor. There are lots of nuances to these overlapping experiences. As for the degrees and grades of prayer, the truth is that in her writings she mentions a lot more than four, but Teresa's life and writings represent years of practicing prayer. Why don't we take this journey one metaphor at a time? For now, make a garden, and be sure that it is getting enough water.

4

Get to Know Yourself

"We can say beginners in prayer are those who draw water from the well; this is a lot of work."

When I was sixteen years old, I decided I wanted to be what the old church mothers in my Church of God in Christ congregation called a "prayer warrior." I had no insight into what exactly made a person a prayer warrior, and I assumed I had to pray a really, really long time to reach my goal. I've never been a morning person, but I sacrificially set my alarm clock to 5:00 AM, determined to pray for two hours before I got ready to go to school.

Beginning seemed easy enough. I started with my standard "Heavenly Father, I come to you in Jesus' name," followed by some familiar praises such as "Lord, you're good. You woke me up this morning, and started me on my way. You made a way out of no way." These were the things we said in church, especially those old church mothers.

I think I asked for a few things. Maybe I asked for a lot of things, not just for myself, but for other people, too. About five minutes into it I'd exhausted my entire repertoire of congregational praises, as well as petitions, and I was left with my thoughts.

Oh my. Where did they come from? Their vast numbers, fracturing into a million directions (when I wasn't slapping my cheeks to stay awake), appalled me. I had to do something!

Like a good Charismatic, I resorted to "praying in the Spirit," which meant I spent what felt like an excruciatingly long time speaking in tongues. I have nothing against the gift of tongues, but the fact is, I had no idea what I was saying. That left me to desperately wage a battle with my mind: *I'm sleepy. I shouldn't be thinking about being sleepy. The basement floor*—where I prayed—*is cold. My knees hurt. What am I going to eat for breakfast? I shouldn't be thinking about breakfast while I'm praying. I'm praying in tongues. Am I really praying in tongues if I'm thinking?* It went on and on, with me thinking, trying not to think, and flogging myself for thinking.

Those two-hour stretches didn't feel very beneficial to me. After a few days, crestfallen and discouraged, I gave up the practice altogether. Instead of being a prayer warrior, I became a prayer *worrier*, afraid I'd never learn the art of prayer and berating myself for my inability to settle my mind.

I'm not the only person who's ever been distracted during prayer. Teresa had trouble gathering her faculties. Consider her attention-deficit hit parade:

From *The Interior Castle*: "It seems to me my soul is like a bird flying that doesn't know where to light. All I did was lose a lot of time without becoming any more virtuous, or progressing in any way in prayer."

From her letters: "The imagination and memory can war with each other until the soul is left powerless. . . . They don't rest in anything, but flit from one thing to another. They're like annoying little moths, flying around at night, going from one extreme to another."

And then there's my personal favorite, also found in her letters: "The intellect is so wild it's like a frantic wild man whom no one can tie down."

This concerned Teresa so much that she prayed about it, very poetically, I might add:

When, my God,
Will I see my soul
Joined together
Praising you,
All of my faculties
Enjoying you?
Do not permit, Lord,
My soul to remain broken.
Too often each piece
Goes its own way
Leaving me
Scattered.

Oh, to have had Teresa's insight when I was sixteen. I had no idea, in practical terms, how to gently draw my thoughts back to a place where communing deeply with God was possible. Teresa's advice is golden:

"We can say beginners in prayer are those who draw water from the well. As I said, this is a lot of work on their part. They must wear themselves out trying to recollect their senses. Since they're so used to being distracted, it takes a lot of effort. They need to get used to not caring about what they see and hear while they're spending time in prayer. Instead, in solitude they should reflect on their past. Everyone needs to do this, often. But the extent to which each person must do it varies. In the beginning, this kind of reflection is painful."

Were you expecting her to say that? I wasn't. Not everyone enjoys looking back, especially at aspects of life that are painful. "What good will dredging up all that stuff do?" you may ask. More than you know.

Teresa felt so strongly about self-knowledge that she insisted we never abandon it. "On this journey there are no giant souls without a need to return often to the stage of a suckling infant." Self-knowledge nourishes the soul. If you're still not convinced, she states it even more explicitly: "Along this path, self-knowledge and the thought of one's sins is the bread all palates must be fed with, no matter how delicate they are. They cannot be sustained without this bread."

I have no problem partaking of the bread of life, but the bread of knowledge of me, including my sinfulness, does not sound

like a tasty morsel I'd want to consume on a regular basis.
Obviously Teresa is not expecting us to choke on examinations of
our lives, but she does find it important enough to emphasize.

The wisdom of this teaching can be found in other places
as well. One of the languages of the Akan culture of Ghana is
made entirely of symbols, called Adinkra symbols. My favorite,
Sankofa, is pictured below.

I'll let African American style writer Harriette Cole tell you
about it:

> The Sankofa symbol is most traditionally illustrated
> as a bird standing with feet forward and neck twisted
> around behind. In the bird's beak is an egg, representing
> the essence of its culture. In the Akan alphabet, Sankofa

stands as a symbol harking us to "go back and fetch it." The
broader understanding of this symbol is that it is our duty in
life to stop in our tracks, turn, and look back at our lives and
history; claim the essence of who we are based on that history;
and then turn and walk with grace, strength, and power into
the present and the future.

Like the Akans', Teresa's self-knowledge was more encom-
passing than the myopic lens through which we postmodern
pilgrims view ourselves. For her, self-examination takes in the
whole soul: who we are and how we live. It is the work that
we do to prepare ourselves. Without this holistic approach,
how can we truly give ourselves to God? Consider this passage
(Romans 12:1): "So here's what I want you to do, God helping
you: Take your everyday, ordinary life—your sleeping, eating,
going-to-work, and walking-around life—and place it before
God as an offering."

You can't cut yourself in pieces and only offer the good parts
to God. He wants all of you; the good and the bad parts; your
weaknesses and strengths; the brokenness you don't want anyone
to know about; as well as those things within that are being
marvelously healed. We must be willing to tell the truth about
ourselves: we are made in the image and likeness of God, and
yet, we sin and fall short of his glory. In the truth we find our
liberty. John 8:32 tells us: "If you stick with this, living out what I
tell you, you are my disciples for sure. Then you will experience
for yourselves the truth, and the truth will free you."

How can the truth about ourselves free us? If we allow it, it can humble us. Teresa offers another one of her homey analogies to explain how this works.

"Humility is like a bee, busy making honey in its hive; it's always working. Without humility, everything goes wrong. But don't forget, the bee continually flies away from the beehive to gather nectar from the flowers. And so the soul must fly from self-knowledge to reflect upon the grandeur and majesty of God."

What does this do for the soul? It will show us how impoverished and utterly needy we are. Teresa said, "By gazing at his grandeur, we get in touch with our own lowliness; by looking at his purity, we see how filthy we are. By pondering his humility, we see the lack of our own."

Black looks blacker next to white, and white looks whiter beside black. Looking away from ourselves to God, and then from God back to ourselves, enables us to become more noble people. We can step off the tiny island of "me," where we're prone to endless spiritual belly-button gazing, and all our fears about our worthlessness gather and commiserate.

WITHOUT GUILT

"Oh, God, help me!" Teresa says. "How many souls does the devil beat up this way? And the poor souls think their fears come from humility. They come from not understanding ourselves completely. They're distortions of self-knowledge. I wouldn't be surprised if we never got free from ourselves because of this lack of freedom from ourselves! Set your eyes on Christ."

But what if we feel guilty because thinking of our past, specifically our sins, is not as painful as we think it should be? It's possible that in examining ourselves we'll feel no remorse for certain big-ticket items. This, too, keeps our focus too much on ourselves. I'm not completely unsympathetic. I understand that a lack of compunction, feeling no sorrow or guilt for past sins, can be troubling to some and possibly stand in the way of moving forward, but a lack of contrition doesn't mean your heart is hard. Fortunately, Teresa addressed this. "The surest sign of repentance is an earnest desire to serve God."

I'm not dismissing contrition. A conscience tender with sorrow for sin is a wonderful ally on the spiritual journey. But it's not the sole indicator that you're responding to the working of the Holy Spirit in your life. So, keep your focus on the Lord, and follow his leading, no matter how you feel, and don't worry about guilt feelings or the lack of them in your self-examination. Guilt can sometimes be your wild man trying to run you off the prayer path. Your intellect will try to distract you in a thousand ways. Go back to Teresa's very practical solution and set your eyes on Christ.

Spiritual writer Brennan Manning had a remarkable experience looking at Christ. In 1956, on a frigid February day, Manning was in a Catholic church praying the Stations of the Cross. The Stations—also known as The Way of the Cross—is a classic devotion that focuses on Jesus' final hours. Through a series of fourteen images—most often mounted on the wall of a church—one takes a pilgrimage of prayer. Beginning with Christ being condemned to death, the faithful walk from scene to scene until finally they face an image of the crucified Christ laid in his tomb. While engaged in this practice, Manning had a powerful experience of the personal love of Jesus Christ. "At that moment," he later recalled, "the entire Christian life became for me an intimate, heartfelt relationship with Jesus."

Manning, like Teresa, is talking about a love affair that began for him by praying with images from the life of Christ. Maybe you don't walk the Stations of the Cross. The rosary is also a prayerful walk through the life of Christ. More creative types can pray through his life by making their own images with paints, colored markers, pencils, and crayons. Or you can pray with icons, called "windows to heaven." Not only do the haunting images on icons commemorate the life of Christ, they tell the stories of many other holy people, too.

Teresa wasn't particular about the form your work at this stage of prayer took. What was most important to her was that you were engaging your faculties and dealing with distractions (gently).

So relax. It doesn't matter what tools you rely on in the early stages—it's all fetching water from the well for the health of your growing garden.

"God grant that there is water in it!" says Teresa. "But that doesn't depend on us. All we can do is our share of the work, drawing it, and watering the flowers."

Rest Stop
Journal Your Journey

At this rest stop you'll linger a little longer, and even come back to it again, I hope, several times throughout our journey with Teresa. I suggest that you start a spiritual journal.

Not just a notebook of your thoughts, your journal will be your private prayer space. Think of it as a portable monk's cell, or hermitage. It is for you and God alone.

Journaling is a fine spiritual practice. From Teresa herself, to Augustine who inspired her, all the way down to writers of our time like Frank Laubach, pilgrims have taken time to jot down dispatches from their soul travels. Journaling is a powerful tool for self-examination.

Don't go out and buy anything fancy, unless of course your journal's beauty will inspire you to write in it. I can't tell you how many beautifully bound journals I've purchased that never saw a word of my reflections. If a spiral-bound notebook from a dollar store is what will get you writing, by all means choose that option.

There's no right or wrong way to journal. Don't worry about not knowing how to face the blank page. You're simply going to jot down anything that comes to mind: Scriptures you're reflecting on; prayers and intercessions; thoughts or blessings you're grateful for. You can paste images in your journal that move you, or you can just doodle.

Most of all, use your journal for self-examination. Write honestly about where you are on your journey. Write about the person you want to be, the person you are, and the space between them. You can even write about what it feels like to write.

Whether you spend time dreaming, or accusing yourself, or ruminating, or doing business with God, put yourself on those pages. I think I can safely say that if you're honest and faithful to show up and write, God will surely meet you between the lines.

5

Look for New Growth

"It is important for you to realize you are making progress.
If someone tells a traveler she has taken the wrong road and lost
her way, she begins to wander aimlessly. The constant search for
the right road tires her, wastes her time, and delays her arrival."

G ood news: you are right where you're supposed to
be on this journey. You've begun to water your garden with self-examination. The tools you're using for
that watering are like a gardener and her bucket. You've begun
to carry a bucket, to use it with great care and attention, and
your prayer life will begin to grow from these ways that you are
nourishing it.

Teresa knew from experience that people don't all pray in the
same way, just as not every plant in the garden needs the same
amount of moisture. What works for one doesn't necessarily
work for another. We need to try on a few prayer styles to see
what fits. Perhaps you tried keeping a journal and instantly

hated it. In fact, maybe you don't like beginning with self-knowledge at all. You know yourself well enough to be sure that you actually *like* vocal prayer! What if saying the Our Father *works* for you, and you wish I'd stop implying that something is wrong with reciting it.

Don't get me wrong. I'm not saying there's *anything* wrong with vocal (spoken out loud) or mental (recited in your mind) prayer, no matter what prayers you're using, including the spontaneous "I'm just talking to God" kind. Teresa was a fan of vocal prayer herself. It was her experience that once a garden was planted, and it was being carefully tended by regular spiritual practice, spoken prayers could once again come alive!

If you are like me, praying out loud takes on an entirely new and powerful role in your life when you have been paying good attention to the garden in your soul. Let's now try to pray the Our Father in what I would call "Teresa style." As she advises: "When you approach God, try to realize whom you are about to address and continue to do so while you are addressing him. If you had a thousand lives, you would never fully understand why this Lord deserves our behavior toward him, before whom even angels tremble. He orders all things, and he can do all things; with him to will is to perform."

● ● ●

The Our Father à la St. Teresa in Five Easy Steps

1. **Steal away.** "Our Lord teaches us that we should pray this prayer while we're alone, just as he was often alone when he prayed. It's impossible to attend to God, and the world at the same time."

2. **Cut yourself some slack if something's wrong with you.** "In times of sickness, times when our heads are tired and, no matter how hard we try, we cannot concentrate, or times, when for our own good, God allows his servants to suffer . . . she should not worry, for she is not to blame. She should pray as best she can." Just do what you can do.

3. **Beg like a rhythm-and-blues singer.** "Do you think that because we cannot hear him he is silent? He speaks clearly to the heart when we beg him from our hearts to do so." Take the words to the song "Ain't Too Proud to Beg" to heart.

4. **Imagine Jesus himself is teaching you the prayer.** "It would be a good idea to imagine that he has taught this prayer to each and every one of us, individually, and that he is continually teaching it to us." Bring your senses to this exercise. See Jesus, what he's wearing, his expression (loving!). Hear his voice. Ask yourself where you are in your mind's eye. What are you feeling in your body as Jesus teaches you? What's going on in your soul? Don't forget to try to use your sense of smell, and even taste, if you can bring it to this imaginative exercise.

5. **Stay with Jesus.** "The master is never so far away that the-disciple needs to shout in order to be heard. He is always right at our side. If you want to recite the Our Father well, you must not leave the side of the master who taught it to you."

Using these five steps, pray the Our Father aloud. Reflect on your experience after each phrase, or sometimes after a special word. Take your time. You don't have to blaze through it. Enjoy the master teacher, who is delighted to have you as a disciple.

Congratulations! If you prayed with love and reverence, keeping Jesus close, then you are indeed on a path to praying in the way of Teresa, and every aspect of your Christian life will blossom as a result! That felt awesome, didn't it? I wouldn't be surprised if the master gave you a big hug for your effort. Teresa leaves us with a little advice:

"If, while I am speaking with God, I am fully conscious of doing so, and if this is more real to me than the words I am uttering, then I am combining mental and vocal prayer."

What's important is that prayer come alive in our lives, reflecting on the relationship we have with Christ, in us. Living prayer with a living God! If this feels fresh to you, like morning sunshine, that may be because prayer is becoming real. It's alive and ripe with awareness of God's presence.

How Do You Feel?

Does it matter how we *feel* in prayer? This would be a good time to talk about consolations, and there are two kinds. You could say that consolations are the warm fuzzies we feel in prayer. The first kind comes from us. For me, it feels like I'm beginning to fall in love, but the object of my affection is God. The other kind of consolation is the kind that comes from God. It's like that big hug from the master you may have felt after you prayed the Our Father so beautifully. It's what you feel when you realize—oh, wonder of wonders— that God is actively, continuously, unrelentingly falling in love with you! It's an extraordinarily good feeling, this kind of consolation.

But—and this is a really big "but" I put it in italics—we can't forget that in this stage, we're doing the work. There's something about feeling that everything relies on your own efforts that's just plain hard. Keep in mind: even the simplest ways of praying with attention can take a lot of energy. You'll get tired. It's just gonna happen. At some point if you continue on this journey, it's inevitable that you'll come to a thin place: an unsettling stage that exists in some hazy realm somewhere between bringing water from the well and turning the crank on the waterwheel. And what happens there and then?

It's unpleasant. Of course you and I both know that we don't feel warm consolation at all times. The rosy feel of good prayer and communion with God isn't constant. Not at all! At times you'll feel confused. The consolations that gave wings to your soul may suddenly be conspicuously absent. After such a delicious foretaste of the divine, the well will run dry.

Teresa asks, "What will these gardeners do if after many days there's nothing but dryness, distaste, vapidness, and a total lack of desire to come draw water?"

She's not just speculating. Teresa experienced aridity for twenty years, when only the thought that what she was doing served and pleased the Lord of the garden kept her from giving up. Listen to her wisdom:

"These labors take their toll. I suffered these trials for many years, and I know they're extraordinary. Whenever I was able to get a drop of water from the sacred well, I thought God was granting me a favor. It seems to me that more courage is needed to do this work than many worldly labors combined. But I have seen clearly that God doesn't leave a single one, even in this lifetime, without a generous reward."

Teresa cautioned us weary bucket-carriers that often we will find that we can't so much as lift our arms, or form a good thought in our heads.

Weariness happens. So rest. Teresa assures us, "God is so good that when for reasons that only he knows—maybe for our own good—the well is dry, he sustains the garden without water and grows our virtue flowers anyway. Like good gardeners, we have to continue to do whatever is in our power, and leave the rest to him."

But it's awful to feel helpless, isn't it? It's hard to trust God when we feel nothing in prayer, and words and images fail us. Lord, have mercy. In those times we just want to give up, mid-prayer.

"Pay no attention," Teresa says, "to that feeling you get of wanting to leave off in the middle of your prayer, but praise the Lord that you desire to pray; you can be assured it comes from your will, which loves to be with God. . . . On occasion, when you find yourself oppressed in that way, try to go to someplace where you can see the sky, and walk up and down a little: that won't interfere with your prayer. After all, you're only human. Don't strain yourself too much."

Once you've taken a walk in the sun, have a try at praying again, if only to please the Beloved. He will not forget what you've done, or you. Trust him.

Rest Stop

Being with the Beloved

On those hard days, when you are a little lost, it helps to have some easy-to-follow instructions. They can simplify what you may be needlessly complicating in the way that you are doing or imagining things, and put you right back on track.

Try these, from wise Teresa:

Teresa's Easy Instructions for Being with the Beloved

Place yourself in the presence of Christ.

Don't wear yourself out thinking.

Simply speak with your Beloved.

Delight in him.

Lay your needs at his feet.

Acknowledge that he doesn't have to allow you to be in his presence.

(But he does!)

There is a time for thinking,

and a time for being.

Be.

With him.

6

Cranking It Up!

"I've explained how the gardener waters his garden through hard work, using his own strength to draw water from a well. Now let's speak of the second method, turning the crank of a waterwheel and drawing the water through an aqueduct. The gardener gets more water for less work and can rest more without having to work constantly. Here the soul begins to be recollected. It happens supernaturally. The soul cannot make this happen by its own efforts. Grace reveals itself."

When Teresa was a child, a picture of Jesus speaking to the Samaritan woman at the well hung on the wall in her room. Later in life she always carried around a small picture of the woman inscribed with the words, "Lord, give me to drink." When she founded her first convent, she constructed a well on the property and called it "the Fountain of the Samaritan Woman."

The woman at the well (her name is Photini, according to tradition) inspires me, too, and the idea of a bucket, a well, and a thirst for God always conjures for me the almost romantic biblical story of her conversion told in the Gospel of John, chapter 4. I can imagine the tenderness in Jesus' eyes when he told her, "If you knew the generosity of God and who I am, you would be asking me for a drink, and I would give you fresh, living water."

Did you ever notice in that story that Photini didn't exactly jump at the chance to partake of this refreshing drink?

Besides stating the obvious, "Sir," she said, "you don't even have a bucket to draw with, and this well is deep," she interrogated him: "So how are you going to get this living water?" It's possible that she put her hand on her hip with this challenge. "Are you a better man that our ancestor Jacob, who dug this well and drank from it, he and his sons and livestock, and passed it down to us?"

Jesus didn't let her resistance sway him and offered her an even more compelling incentive. "Everyone who drinks this water will get thirsty again and again. Anyone who drinks the water I give will never thirst—not ever. The water I give will be an artesian spring within, gushing fountains of endless life."

I believe that nestled within this conversation are several valuable truths. Let's go back for a moment to Teresa's metaphor: this water is prayer. What if everything Jesus said about water in this encounter could also apply to prayer? It certainly wouldn't be the first New Testament story with multiple applications. Indulge me.

The first thing I believe this story teaches is about contemplative prayer, and this is something Teresa knew: it's a gift. Jesus mentions the generosity of God, and the fact that he would *give* her fresh, living water; she wouldn't have to earn it.

This conversation, so enigmatic to the Samaritan woman and maybe even to us, also suggests that a certain degree of humility is necessary to receive this gift. You have to *know* the generosity of God, as Jesus suggested, and be willing to receive it. Teresa has said: "You would not be humble if God were to offer you a favor and you refused to accept it. You would show humility by accepting it, and being pleased with it, yet realizing how far you are from deserving it."

The story also hints at the fact that a relationship with Christ is central. Jesus said if she knew who he was, she would have asked him for the water. That implies we'll get this water as a result of our relationship with Jesus.

Finally, we can't forget the sheer volume of the water Jesus spoke of. These weren't little trickles. He mentioned gushing. And fountains. Don't miss their location either: inside—they're within us.

Let's face it, at this stage in our prayer journeys, we're not exactly gushing fountains of endless life. Sure, we've said prayers with awareness and love. Christ has taught us how to pray, and we've tried our best to keep him with us. Sometimes, we've simply *been* with him, telling him our needs, being thankful that he allows wretches like us to approach him. We've examined ourselves, found ourselves wanting, and changed in response to the grace that prayer brings to our lives.

The changes are nothing dramatic. We aren't levitating or being shocked by burning bushes chatting with us. It's in the little things that God is revealing himself to us. We catch whispers of his voice through our spiritual reading, or in sermons we hear, or woven throughout conversations with the people who guide our souls. And deep within, we feel God beckoning us to come closer.

Everyone who endeavors to pray begins this way. After a while we get used to it, but that doesn't particularly free us from the challenges we face when we build a habit of prayer. Distractions still assail us. Maybe like Teresa, we wish we could go off to some secluded place, permanently, just so we can seek God.

She once said, "I began to envy those who live in deserts. I thought since they didn't hear or see anything they were free of wandering minds. What I heard was, 'You are greatly mistaken, daughter. For them, the temptations of the devil there are stronger. Be patient with yourself. For as long as you live, you won't be able to avoid a wandering mind.'"

By now we've probably realized our gardens are a wee bit bigger than they seemed at first. They're vast, in fact, and still undernourished, although we've made an impressive effort to take care of them. Our arms are tired; maybe they're tired a lot of the time. But we can't give up and go back to how we lived before. There are still patches of dry and barren soil in our gardens, and many virtues must be nurtured in order to bloom.

Oh, Lord, we need more water! Even if we're full of resistance like the woman at the well, we're also, like her, thirsty. So we stay at that well talking to Jesus, bucket in hand, trying to wrap our minds around what he's really offering.

If we stay there long enough, Jesus' love compels us until, like Photini, we finally yield and say, "Sir, give me this water so I won't ever get thirsty, won't ever have to come back to this well again."

But wait! He didn't just hand it over. "Go call your husband and then come back," he said.

"I have no husband."

"Nicely put: 'I have no husband.' You've had five husbands, and the man you're living with now isn't even your husband. You spoke the truth there, sure enough."

Ouch! He certainly flipped the situation. It's a little painful to read how he called her out.

Photini immediately acknowledged that Jesus was a prophet, but confronted with her sins she seemed to forget all about the water; she wanted to talk theology! Which you have to admit is a great way to get out of dealing with your sins. Jesus didn't banish her for such useless deflection. He engaged her and answered her questions. Not only that, he was kind enough to reveal who he is to her: the Messiah. Then he told her something interesting, "It's who you are and the way you live that count before God. Your worship must engage your spirit in the pursuit of truth. That's the kind of people the Father is out looking for: those who are simply and honestly themselves before him in their worship. God is sheer being itself—Spirit. Those who worship him must do it out of their very being, their spirits, their true selves, in adoration."

This is a valuable lesson about prayer, my fellow pilgrims. It suggests that we must live honest, examined lives. The water of prayer, especially contemplative prayer, demands transparency in us. Pure water, held up to the light, makes our dust and tiny particles of debris entirely visible.

God is love, and if he shows us our sins, he gives us the grace to repent. Remember what Teresa said—in the quote that opens this chapter—about the second way of drawing water, when it flows more effortlessly, and how it is in this way that grace reveals itself?

When Jesus confronted Photini, grace was revealing itself with such clarity it discombobulated her. She walked away from him confused, leaving her water pot—her bucket—behind. And isn't that an interesting metaphor for us to ponder?

Will you leave the work of prayer behind when confronted with your sins?

We may have less work in this kind of prayer, but we still have work, and it includes the difficult labor of taking hard looks at ourselves.

When Jesus met Photini, he asked her to give him a drink. He wasn't even supposed to talk to her! I believe he was asking, in some small way, for her to welcome him or to serve him in friendship. Cleaning your spiritual house of the smudges of sin is a gesture of friendship, service, and welcome for the divine guest. Do it not because you're proud and don't want him to see you so raggedy. Tidy your house because you love him and want him to have a lovely visit with you.

So far on this prayer pilgrimage we've been focusing on becoming good companions for God. We've learned to recollect ourselves, to quiet our faculties—which is still mostly of our own doing. Think of a hedgehog curling up, or a turtle drawing into its shell. These creatures draw inward whenever they want to, as do we. We can do that.

But the kind of contemplative prayer that Teresa is guiding us into next is what Teresa sometimes calls "the prayer of quiet," meaning that we don't do the work, other than to quiet ourselves so that God can speak through and in us. We don't withdraw when we want to; we do so when God grants us this gift. It's like being called by Jesus away from preparing the house to sit at his feet. In the prayer of quiet the master gardener calls us to rest from watering the garden, and we go to him. How can we resist such a compelling call? We find ourselves enveloped in his arms, which is our soul's repose, and we rest.

Teresa offers yet another beautiful analogy: "It is a state in which the soul enters into peace, or rather, in which the Lord gives it peace through his presence, as he did the just man Simeon."

Have you ever read that story in Luke 2:21–34? Jesus' parents take him to Jerusalem to give him to God as a holy offering.

In Jerusalem at the time, there was a man, Simeon by name, a good man, a man who lived in the prayerful expectancy of help for Israel. And the Holy Spirit was on him. The Holy Spirit had shown him that he would see the Messiah of God before he died. Led by the Spirit, he entered the Temple. As the parents of the child Jesus brought him in to carry out the rituals of the Law, Simeon took him into his arms and blessed God:

> "God, you can now release your servant;
> release me in peace as you promised.
> With my own eyes I've seen your salvation;
> it's now out in the open for everyone to see:
> A God-revealing light to the non-Jewish nations,
> and of glory for your people Israel."

All Simeon did was take the child in his arms. It was the infant Christ who revealed who he was. All you have to do is take Christ in your arms, welcoming him into your world. Bless him like Simeon did, and he will release you to peace. Grace takes over. And how do you bless him? In prayer, using whatever form suits you best—praying the words that God will give you.

In the beginning of contemplative prayer, the faculties still. The soul realizes, without knowing how it happened, that it's suddenly very close to God. If it were a teeny bit closer it would be one with God! It may only last a few moments, but it's oh-so-real. Can you see why we have to do some business with God before he comes to us this way? It's so intimate. Even Teresa believed, "When His Majesty grants it, he does so to people who are already beginning to despise the things of the world."

Her audience was primarily nuns, but she made allowances for more complicated lives, like ours are today. "He calls such people to give their attention to interior matters," she counsels. And thank God, attention is what he wants most.

We may not be able to abandon our lives and run off to monasteries to live in perfect contemplation, but we can and should attend, with great love, to our souls. Or rather, we should simply attend to Christ. Teresa believed, "If we desire to make room for His Majesty, he will not only give us this but more, calling us all to advance further."

Our attention will wander off—of course it will!—but that doesn't mean that God's grace will stop revealing itself to us. Teresa says that those crazy mental wild men will return from time to time, and the intellect and memory can still wander off, but she emphasizes a playful, gentle approach to dealing with them:

"When you find yourself in this state of prayer and the under-standing wanders off in search of the most ridiculous things in the world, you should laugh at it and treat it like the silly thing it is. Stay in your state of quiet. Your thoughts will come and go, but the will is an all-powerful mistress and will recall them without your having to worry about it."

So don't worry. If you're experiencing the "prayer of quiet," even for an instant, you're already on the boat, moving forward.

"The sea voyage can be made," Teresa says. "We should not travel too slowly. We need to consider the ways we can get accustomed to these good habits. Souls who do so are more protected from many occasions of sin, and the fire of divine love is readily ignited in them. They are so near the flames that, however little the understanding has fanned the fire, any small spark that flies out at them will cause them to combust. When it is not hindered from the outside, the soul remains alone with its God and is thoroughly prepared to ignite."

Catch afire, gentle pilgrim. Catch afire with divine love.

What if this gift of contemplation hasn't visited you yet? Or you're not quite ready to explode with love? Maybe you should change tactics. Once your Martha work is done and your spiritual house is clean, be like Mary and simply sit down and enjoy the guest. Quietly wait. Here, less is more. Teresa says, "In this work of the spirit the one who thinks less and has less desire to act does more. What we must do is beg like the needy poor before a rich and powerful emperor. Then lower our eyes and humbly wait."

Rest Stop
A Final Examen

Here's another spiritual practice that may help you along the way, as you walk with Teresa.

What student hasn't trembled at the thought of final examinations? They're important. Not only are they a large part of academic grades, but they're indicators of what we've learned—what we know. But examination and examen are not the same thing. I love the way that Richard Foster, in his wonderful book *Prayer: The Heart's True Home*, clarifies the difference. He acknowledges that examination and examen carry much of the same meaning, sans the academic context. But examen refers to the tongue, or a weight indicator, or a balancing scale. It indicates the idea of "an accurate assessment of the true situation." The truth will set you free, including the truth of where we are spiritually on any given day.

Ignatius Loyola thought daily examen so important that he urged his followers, the Jesuits, to do it if all other prayers for the day were abandoned. Some people do this hourly, but why don't we start off by trying it tonight before we go to sleep, and if you want to continue to do it until it's a daily habit, well, amen!

There are two aspects of this kind of prayer, which Foster likens to two sides of a door. On the first side of the door is an examen of consciousness. Here we look at how God has been present to us throughout the day, and how we've responded to his loving presence. The second is an examen of conscience. We take an honest look at our failures, weaknesses, and faltering, to discover where we need to be cleansed and made whole.

Try these five simple reflections based on Ignatius Loyola's Daily Examen, and give the same attention to them as you did to the Lord's Prayer. Take your time. The only place you're going after this is to sleep. And hey, it beats, "If I should die before I wake, I pray the Lord my soul to take."

1. **Ask God to be with you.** Some people light a candle to remind them that he is the light and they rely on him to illuminate his movements in their life. Imagine Christ has stood beside you all day; his hand, comforting and protecting, rests on your shoulder. Do you see him? Did you acknowledge him in any way? How did you respond to his constant presence? Remember, examen isn't about just what you did right or wrong. What can some of the lessons of seeing Christ with you throughout your day teach you about yourself?

2. **Give thanks.** While it's a good exercise to count blessings instead of sheep, giving thanks entails more. Each time I pray the divine office it includes Psalm 95.

This praise psalm welcomes the faithful to pray, but I believe it serves a dual purpose. When we pray words such as "Come let us worship and bow down, bending the knee before our maker," it points us to the truth of our relationship with a great and mighty God. Giving thanks becomes an act of worship and gives us another opportunity to be grateful that he is with us.

3. **Take a look.** At your day, yourself, and once again at Christ present in your life, not necessarily in that order. Where did you get it right? Where did you mess up? Don't be afraid to go deeper, focusing a microscope on not just your behavior but also your motivations. Ask yourself questions like, "Am I where God wants me to be? Should I continue what I'm doing? Or go in another direction? What issues have I let stand between me and the grace God freely offers?" Be unswervingly honest. No one is privy to this examen but you and God. Remember love himself supports you.

4. **Ask for forgiveness.** "I am sorry" are three very difficult words for some to say. "I have sinned" is an even harder admission, but these words are very healing if you allow the grace that comes with them to nourish your soul. Remember that Teresa said self-knowledge and the thought of our sins is bread for every palate, no matter how delicate. This exercise is not permission to judge yourself harshly but, rather, to energize and strengthen you for the journey.

It gives a whole new spin to "give us this day our daily bread." Trust your Father to forgive you your trespasses, while you forgive a few yourself.

5. **Have hope.** Again, examen is not just about what we've done, right or wrong; it's about seeing God with us. God with us adds muscle to our faith. It stirs our love, not just for him but for others, and softens our hearts to be servants of love. It offers the prospect of seeing another day as bright, shiny, and full of possibilities.

Psalm Prayer

Psalm 139:23–24

Investigate my life, O God,
find out everything about me;
Cross-examine and test me,
get a clear picture of what I'm about;
See for yourself whether I've done anything wrong—
then guide me on the road to eternal life.

VERY LITTLE IS NEEDED TO MAKE A HAPPY LIFE

7

The Glorious Foolishness

"Now let's speak about the third water that nourishes this garden,
which is water flowing from a river or stream.
This method requires much less labor, although some work is
involved to direct the flow to the right channel. The Lord desires
to help the gardener so much here that he practically becomes the
gardener himself; the One who does everything."

I n the last chapter, we heard of what Teresa sometimes
calls "the second degree of prayer," likened to turning the
crank of a waterwheel and drawing the water through an
aqueduct. In this kind of praying:

- We do less of the work.
- God grants the soul "the prayer of quiet." This is the beginning
  of contemplative prayer. It's a gift of God-infused peace that
  only lasts a few moments, and it is often granted to those

who have already begun to care less for the things of the world. Our will is occupied while we pray, but it doesn't know how.

- We can't make the "prayer of quiet" happen, but we can position ourselves to receive it.
- We still battle distractions.

Now, we're going to transition from working hard in our gardens to enjoying watching the master gardener work on our behalf.

Teresa's way of contemplative prayer, where it is God praying in and through you, takes some getting used to! This is new territory for most of us.

When contemplation is in full mode, Teresa says, "In this prayer, the faculties fall asleep. They don't stop functioning completely, but they don't understand how they're functioning. The consolations, sweetness, and delights the soul experiences are incomparably greater and more pleasurable than those experienced in the previous prayer. The water of grace has risen as high as the soul's neck, leaving it powerless. It can't go forward; it doesn't know how! Nor can it move backward."

Even our guide has trouble articulating what this experience is like. "I don't know any other way to describe it, or how to explain it. The soul isn't much help. It doesn't know whether to speak or be silent, to laugh or to weep. This prayer is a glorious foolishness, a heavenly madness in which one learns true wisdom. For the soul, it's a most delightful fulfillment."

The Beloved draws very close to the soul here, and the soul responds, wanting to be with him so badly that nothing else matters. Have you ever felt that way?

Teresa says, "This person is like a man already holding a funeral candle in his hand, on the verge of dying the death he's been longing for. His agony holds unutterable delight. It seems to me this experience is nothing other than an almost complete death to all earthly things, and a consuming enjoyment of God."

Uh-oh. Did you hear that noise? It was the sound of many pilgrims closing this book. Dying to even a few earthly things, much less to all of them, is not a popular topic, even for Christians. The thought of letting go of everything can cause some of us to panic. We think we'll die not only to the things of this world, but also to "us"—our essential selves.

● ● ●

I was in counseling years ago with a wonderful psychologist. For weeks I was full of angst and self-loathing. I wanted to be anyone but me at this time, or so I thought. During one session, she finally asked me, "Who would you like to be?"

She threw me off completely. I stammered. "Wha—*what*? I don't want to be anyone else!"

My therapist chuckled. "Isn't it amazing how much self-preservation people have, even when they don't realize they have it?"

No, we don't want to die, not to our stuff, and not to ourselves, or what we perceive as ourselves, which is tangled with our attachments. We rage, rage against the living in the light. And the guy with the funeral candle was just Teresa's metaphor! Jesus' words are even more challenging.

Listen carefully: "Unless a grain of wheat is buried in the ground, dead to the world, it is never any more than a grain of wheat. But if it is buried, it sprouts and reproduces itself many times over. In the same way, anyone who holds on to life just as it is destroys that life. But if you let it go, reckless in your love, you'll have it forever, real and eternal" (John 12:24–25).

I have to admit I'm a little relieved after reading that. There's something about the idea of letting go in reckless love that softens the idea of the dying to all my attachments. I don't feel like I and everything I love are about to be eradicated. Maybe because something in me knows love—and God is love— doesn't destroy us; love frees us to be who we are meant to be in Christ. In fact, here "death" is really surrender—giving our whole selves to God until we are in the world, but not of it.

I learned a little about this kind of surrender on Easter Sunday in 2004. I stole away from my family and went to see Mel Gibson's movie *The Passion of the Christ*, alone. I wanted it to be an experience I shared only with my Beloved. I had no idea what I was about to get myself into.

Mercy! That was the most graphic depiction of the Lord's Passion that I'd ever encountered, and I'd seen some hardcore ones as a kid when I read those Jack T. Chick evangelical fundamentalist comics. But this was altogether different. The movie affected me so deeply that I cried the whole time I watched it, all the way back home in my car, and—I'm not exaggerating—every time I thought of it—which was often—for the next three days. It was the closest thing I've ever felt to Teresa's experience of seeing the statue of the suffering Christ, *Ecce Homo*.

What I felt was more than pure emotion. I can be a drama queen; I know the difference. The Holy Spirit infused my every thought of that movie and made my experience a prolonged revelation of Jesus' sacrifice. I was given what people in Teresa's day sometimes called the "gift of tears." Teresa said tears gain all things. One water draws down the other. This gift, a special grace that ancient Christians fairly begged for, poured the master gardener's water all over me. The tears almost completely absorbed my senses, but I was still aware to some degree. They didn't obliterate them.

But how did I know I wasn't having a normal emotional response to such brutal images? After all, I cry every year when Frosty the Snowman melts, even though I've watched that cartoon every holiday season since the seventies. The truth is, I didn't know immediately, but later I saw the spiritual fruit that the experience yielded. I was profoundly changed. I told a friend later, "That movie stripped me of ambition."

"What do you mean?" he said, a little concerned. He didn't think I was ambitious enough.

"I don't want anything but Jesus now."

All my dreams dissolved in those tears. What I wanted—all my "me-me-me" stuff—bowed to such astounding grace, and in this fertile time of receptiveness when my emotions were so yielded, God could speak to me about a few dreams he had in mind for me. It would have taken me a long time to get there on my own. So it is with the gifts of contemplation. Teresa says, "Work that would take a poor soul twenty years on its own to do to quiet the intellect, this master gardener accomplishes in a moment." Or in my case, in about two hours at the movies, and three or four days afterward.

I don't mean I never had another dream or goal of my own. What I'm getting at is that an indelible impression was made, one that changed the course of my life. My Easter cinematic experience, like Teresa's encounter with the statue, was a second conversion. The master gardener gave me so much water that virtues exploded into bloom—all his doing. Like Teresa, this conversion didn't perfect me, but it certainly set some important things in motion. And I believe there are many more gifts in prayer to come. For me, and for you.

It sounds a little absurd to say a movie changed me, and it sounds kind of nutty to say a statue changed Teresa. That goes to show you that God does things in the way he wants to (which takes the pressure off, when you think about it). We don't have to be veteran pray-ers to experience mind-blowing encounters with God.

• • •

When I was fifteen years old I was "born again." I've mentioned that I wanted to be just like the old church mothers. After my conversion, their great expectation was for me to be filled with the Holy Ghost—we didn't say Holy Spirit back then.

I didn't know exactly what being filled with the Holy Ghost was, but if God was going around filling people with anything, I wanted him to fill me, too. I'd have done whatever it took to position myself to receive such a gift. The church mothers said I had to tarry, or wait for this gift. (Sounds a lot like the way we have to wait for the gift of contemplative prayer to me.)

There were many ways to tarry, from what I could tell. Most of them involved worship, praise, and humbly petitioning God for the gift. And, of course, waiting. If I didn't see immediate results I was to continue worshiping, praising, and asking from a sincere heart. And waiting. Fortunately most of that could be done right there at church.

Maybe it's because I was fifteen and naïve about most things in life, but I had no doubt whatsoever that God would fill me if I asked him to. I knew it was possible that he wouldn't. Even in the few days since I'd been born again I'd hung around long enough to catch a few war stories of people who did not, despite their most arduous efforts at having faith, receive this gift. They tarried every week! But it didn't matter to me if I had to wait a very long time for the Holy Ghost. I was willing.

On a crisp April night, a few days after my born-again experience, I went to church to tarry. The presence of the Lord was almost palpable. Turns out I didn't have to wait very long.

Right after the sermon the evangelist had a prayer line, and he laid hands on everyone who came forward. I didn't know what anyone else prayed for as they filed, one by one, before him. I just knew they looked like they were having what Teresa would have called a "glorious foolish" time. My hope became singular. I only wanted one thing from God, and this gift was so close I could almost taste it.

By the time I got to the front of the line my heart was so wide open I don't think the preacher had to touch me. But he did, and when he placed his hand on my head it felt as though warmth opened up my skull and something that felt like pure love poured inside of me. From the top of my head, all the way down to my feet, and back up again. My entire being was swept into worship, and for the next few hours—we were Pentecostals—my soul was a slave to praise.

Teresa described it like this: "A person utters innumerable praises to God without thinking, unless the Lord does the thinking. The intellect is worthless here. All the soul wants is to cry out praises; it's beside itself in delightful disquiet. Now the flowers are blooming and beginning to spread their fragrance. The soul wishes everyone could see and understand the glory of God and share in the joy. I think it's like the woman in the Gospels who lost her coin. When she'd found it, she had to call her neighbor, her joy was so complete."

The woman who found her lost coin comes from Luke 15:8–10: "Imagine a woman who has ten coins and loses one. Won't she light a lamp and scour the house, looking in every nook and cranny until she finds it? And when she finds it you can be sure she'll call her friends and neighbors: 'Celebrate with me! I found my lost coin!' Count on it—that's the kind of party God's angels throw every time one lost soul turns to God."

The first thing the woman did was light a lamp. I didn't have to do that. God illuminated me when he drew me to Jesus. I also didn't sweep my own house clean. All my sins were forgiven at my conversion. The searching every nook and cranny was taken care of both through my initial conversion combined with my earnest seeking. I was a brand new convert, too inexperienced to do anything but let the master gardener do most of the work. He made it possible for me to find my coin. And when I found it, I did tell everyone who would listen. If only my high school's office would have handed over the public address system! I'd have reached far more than the few dozen people I told the next day.

Teresa understood contemplative prayer as all God's doing. One of the great Christian teachers of prayer in our lifetime, the Cistercian monk and abbot Thomas Keating, agrees. He says in no uncertain terms, "Contemplative prayer is considered to be the pure gift of God. It is the opening of mind and heart—our whole being—to God, the ultimate mystery, beyond thoughts, words, and emotions. Through grace we open our awareness to God who we know by faith is within us, closer than breathing, closer than thinking, and closer than choosing—closer than the subconscious itself."

Still, we have to prepare ourselves to receive and understand the gift. That's what the previous chapters were all about. The method of preparing yourself for the gift of contemplative prayer is not the gift itself; it's simply what opens you up to receive it. Think of a journey. The journey is not the destination: it's the way you get there. The destination is where you arrive at the end of your journey. They're not the same thing.

This third degree of prayer is where we change our whole approach. We move from activity to receptivity. Just as I did at fifteen, we open ourselves so God can fill us. And just like the church mothers taught me way back when, a fine place to begin is asking for the gift, and waiting.

For a few moments, set your bucket down. Simply open your heart, and wait for the master gardener. He wants to come and relieve you of so much work. Let him.

Rest Stop
Contemplative Listening

Y ou may have heard the term *lectio divina*. I don't
want to throw a lot of new concepts at you all
at once—but this one is important. This spiritual
practice will help you to become more receptive and ready
for contemplative prayer.

Lectio divina means "divine reading," but don't let that
simple definition fool you. *Lectio* is a weighty spiritual
discipline. It comes from the ancient prayer tradition called
haggadah, an interactive interpretation of the Scriptures. In
this method you listen to the Word of God in Scripture to
deepen your friendship with Christ.

Imagine you're having an intimate conversation with
your Beloved. You're completely attuned to him, but he
suggests the topics. Spending time with him this way, so
actively engaged in reading his Word, moves you beyond a
mere acquaintanceship and cultivates love and trust. Soon,
instead of merely enjoying a conversation, you'll find that
you are intimately sharing with Christ. It's a wonderful way
to prepare your heart for the gift of contemplation.

The First Moment
Lectio (Read)

Read the Scripture passage for the first time. Listen with your interior ears—the ears of your heart, so to speak. Ask yourself if any words, phrases, or sentences resonate with you. If so, repeat them over and over until they settle deep within your heart. If you were enjoying a fine meal, this would be like taking your first few bites. Savor the meal—the soul food—and return to your word, phrase, or sentence until you feel it's a part of you.

The Second Moment
Meditatio (Reflect)

Reflect on the words until they resound in your heart. Relish them. This is not just taking a bite of your soul food meal and deeply enjoying it. It's swallowing it. Let your attitude be one of quietness and receptivity. Listen attentively to what speaks to your heart.

The Third Moment
Oratio (Respond)

Respond spontaneously as you listen to your words, phrase, or sentence. Prayers of praise, thanksgiving, and even petition may arise. You could liken this to lavishly expressing your gratitude to the master chef for such a fine meal, before you're even finished eating.

The Fourth Moment
Contemplatio (Rest)

Rest in God. Simply "be with" him. Here you sigh with contentment after you've eaten, and spend the rest of your time enjoying God's company. Teresa would say the soul goes about like a person "whose appetite is satisfied and who has no need to eat." But it is not so full that it couldn't be tempted to savor a little dessert if you stirred its appetite. This "being with" the Beloved is as much a part of the meal as the food itself; it's the difference between dining together and communing.

8

Holy Longing

*"Nothing compares to the delight the Lord desires
a soul to enjoy in this our exile."*

I remember the first time I tried contemplative prayer. I told my spiritual director, Amy, that I felt drawn to it. At the time I had a lot of noise going on in my head—more than usual.

Amy gave me a pamphlet with the basic information about centering prayer, one of the most popular ways of learning contemplative prayer. A few days later I tried it for the first time. As the pamphlet instructed, I chose a word, the symbol of my intention to consent to the presence of God and his action within me. Being the love bug I like to think I am, I picked the word *love*.

Next I found a comfortable seat and started to become aware of my breathing as I began to quiet down. Ah, yes. This was going to be marvelous. Very casually I introduced my word: "Love."

Absolutely nothing happened, which was fine. I tried it again, slowly and meditatively this time. "Looooooove."

That didn't do much for me either. Already I was bored to death. But the third time's the charm, right? Once again:

"Loooooooooooove . . ."

"Chatterchatterchatterchatterchatter!" That was the full frontal assault of my monkey mind. As usual. Before I started what I hoped would become a daily practice, I'd already imagined how my mind would pose a challenge to me hearing God in this way.

As it was, I had raging symptoms of attention deficit disorder, although my doctor refused to diagnose me with it because I couldn't produce a report card from second grade to prove I had had it as a child. I couldn't find my shoes most days! Even *quiet* distracted me. So I expected some difficulty with the mental debris that usually rushed through the stream of my consciousness. But surely I could hold my thoughts at bay for a brief twenty-minute session. I was a grown woman!

I lasted ten minutes. Tops.

Thomas Keating would say the monkey chatter was an integral part of the process. All I had to do was notice and disregard it, just as I would the sappy easy listening music that's background noise in the grocery store. I was to return to my sacred word, and by it, to my Beloved. Gently. In fact, Keating would have encouraged me to have a friendly, joyful attitude toward my monkey chatter, including the worst of the thoughts that emerged. But I didn't trust such a winsome way of dealing with my faculties. I returned to my standard attempt at monkey wrestling.

I tried to force myself not to think, which made me think about not thinking until I became obsessed with it; then I became *distressed* by it! Seconds dragged on like minutes, thinking of not thinking, and minutes like hours until I realized I'd rather stab myself in the hand with a rusty fork than continue that futile attempt for twenty eternal minutes.

During my next visit with Amy she asked me how it all went—the contemplative prayer experiment. I mumbled something like, "I don't think centering prayer is for me." She gave me a sly smile, neither concerned nor surprised. We both knew I simply wasn't ready, not yet, and that was okay.

I read a lot of books about prayer while preparing to write this one. For all my research I found that, other than spiritual warfare prayers, contemplative prayer was the only other method that came with warnings. For most people, attempting to enter into interior silence with little experience is intensely uncomfortable. We're clueless as to what to do with our thoughts, to say nothing of how it feels to deal with *all that God*. Richard Foster perhaps put it best when he said, "While we are all equally precious in the eyes of God, we are not equally ready to listen to 'God's speech in his wondrous, terrible, gentle, loving, all embracing silence.'"

As usual, Teresa knew what I needed. It was Teresa who said that the soul becomes "quite a fool" when it tries to induce contemplative prayer on its own. "I can't persuade myself to use my human efforts in a matter in which His Majesty has placed limits. Better to leave the work to him. There are other efforts he didn't reserve for himself: penance, works of charity, and prayer—inasmuch as we can do these things, being as wretched as we are."

Trying to force your mind to go to places God hasn't given it the grace to go is something Teresa cautioned against, even though her stance was in stark contrast to the teachings of many prayer teachers in her day—and in ours. I have to admit, she made a strong case.

TERESA'S FOUR REASONS TO AVOID FORCING THE MIND INTO SUBMISSION

1. **It doesn't work.** She says, "If His Majesty hasn't begun to absorb us, I don't know how the mind can be stopped."

2. **All these inner activities are gentle and serene.** Teresa considered doing anything arduous harmful to the soul, and to her, even holding your breath is arduous. "Leave the soul in God's hands, allowing him to do whatever he wishes with it, showing no interest in how this can benefit you. Resign yourself to God's will."

3. **The harder you try not to think of anything, the more aroused your mind will become** and you'll end up thinking even more. It's a vicious cycle. Teresa said, "The important thing is not to think much, but love much, and do whatever stirs you to love."

4. **It's not about you.** Teresa says, "What is most essential and pleasing to God is that we are aware of his glory, and forget about ourselves, what profits us, comforts us, and delights us." How can we forget ourselves when we are being obsessively careful not to stir our minds or desire? We can't. Besides, according to Teresa such stirrings can actually awaken powerful longing for God.

All this reminds me of a passage from the Song of Songs 8:4: "Don't excite love, don't stir it up, until the time is ripe—and you're ready."

Contemplation is, literally, being in *love*, and God himself is the love we're in. Attempting to dive into this kind of prayer before you're ready—before you can handle the awesome silence of God—is like stirring love before its time. If you've ever been in love, you know it's demanding. I don't mean falling in love. That's a lot easier for many of us. But sustaining a relationship, even with God—staying in love—costs. We pay with our time, commitment, humility, endurance, fidelity, and a host of other things you may not have anticipated in the falling-in-love phase.

In this third degree of prayer you go beyond the holy idleness of Mary, sitting at Christ's feet, gazing at him with wonder shining in your eyes. Teresa says that here the soul "can also be Martha in such a way that it's as if it's engaged in the active and contemplative life together." In other words, your experience of God's love through the gift of contemplative prayer should result in wanting to share that love in practical ways with others. You may have a sudden urge to buy groceries for a needy neighbor, or to volunteer at the local soup kitchen. Or you may begin visiting sick members of your church to encourage them. Active work will rise from your interior work, just as lovely, fragrant flowers emerge from a root. They'll proceed from the rich soil of God's love, and we'll do those deeds for him alone, without a whit of self-interest.

But don't expect that you won't feel in any way conflicted, even doing good works. Teresa says the soul in this state "takes care of those less fortunate, and tends to business. It reads good books, but it isn't master of itself. It understands the best part of the soul is elsewhere. It's like speaking to someone at our side, but from the other side someone else is speaking. We can't give either conversation our full attention."

This kind of prayer fills a soul with holy longing that both wounds and heals us. It wounds because we can't be with our Beloved the way we desire to. It heals us because the longing ultimately draws us to the very union we crave. The soul remains in the world with a hunger or a gnawing ache that can't be satisfied, except by full union with God. It's a little complicated, because despite the soul's longing, God still grants the gift according to his will. In her autobiography, Teresa complained that as a busy abbess, she felt she had too little time for contemplation, and in the times she did her Beloved seemed to play hide-and-seek. She asked him, "How is this compatible with your mercy?" Then she boldly asserted, "If it were possible for me to hide from you, as it is for you to hide from me, the love you have for me would not allow it. But you're with me, and always see me. Don't allow it!" David writes about holy longing in several psalms, notably Psalm 42:1–3:

A white-tailed deer drinks from the creek;
I want to drink God,
deep draughts of God.
I'm thirsty for God-alive.
I wonder, "Will I ever make it—
arrive and drink in God's presence?"
I'm on a diet of tears—
tears for breakfast, tears for supper.
All day long people knock at my door,
Pestering, "Where is this God of yours?"

Even the prophet Isaiah experienced it:

Through the night my soul longs for you.
Deep from within me my spirit reaches out to you.
(Isaiah 29:6)

I'm grateful that God is merciful. He keeps drawing us to himself. He's also complicated—an understatement, I know. Remember he's the one who offered a Samaritan gal a drink of eternal water, but when she finally asked for it, he told her to go home and deal with her husband who's not her husband. He's the seemingly hide-and-seek lover who exasperates us with what we think are his maddening disappearing acts. How did the

Shulamite woman in the Song of Songs respond to his absence? The way only those deeply in love and full of longing do.

"I died inside. Oh—I felt so bad." Ultimately this death is what brings us even closer to God, because it really isn't death. It's deeper surrender.

Her actions that followed reflect what many of us do when we are filled with holy longing.

> I ran out looking for him,
> But he was nowhere to be found.
> I called into the darkness. But no answer.

Like most of us do in the dark night, she endured many painful trials, with only the memory of his presence to urge her on. But soon she grew weary and begged her sisters for help.

> If you find my lover,
> Please tell him I want him,
> that I'm heartsick with love for him.

Her sisters asked where they can help her find him, and her answer points us back to prayer. "My lover is already on the way to the garden, to browse among the flowers, touching the colors and forms. I am my lover's, and my lover is mine. He caresses the sweet smelling flowers."

He really does love those virtue flowers.

Keep praying, pilgrim. You will always find your Beloved in the garden, even after a dark and painful night of longing for him. We must trust him.

Teresa says, "If he wants to bring the soul to heaven, it goes. If he wants to plunge it into hell, it feels no sorrow because it goes with God. . . . Let His Majesty treat the soul as his own. The soul no longer belongs to itself. It is given entirely to the Lord."

But don't you worry. Eventually his voice will beckon us back to springtime, and we will hear him say sweetly in our souls:

> Get up, my dear friend,
> fair and beautiful lover—come to me!
> Look around you: Winter is over;
> the winter rains are over, gone!
> Spring flowers are in blossom all over.
> The whole world's a choir—and singing!
> Spring warblers are filling the forest
> with sweet arpeggios.
> Lilacs are exuberantly purple and perfumed,
> and cherry trees fragrant with blossoms.
> Oh, get up, dear friend,
> my fair and beautiful lover—come to me!
> Come, my shy and modest dove—
> leave your seclusion, come out in the open.
> Let me see your face,
> let me hear your voice.
> For your voice is soothing
> and your face is ravishing.
> (Song of Songs 2:10–14; 5:4–8; 6:1–3)

And when we hear him, we'll fly into his arms.

Teresa says, "The soul is well aware that this is a joy that cannot be reached by the understanding. The will embraces this joy, without understanding how. However, the soul does understand that this joy is a blessing that could not be gained by all the merits of all the trials on earth. It is a gift from the Lord of heaven and earth, who freely gives it like the God he is. This is perfect contemplation."

It is, indeed, Teresa.

Teresa's Prayer

My king, I beg you,

Make everyone I speak to mad with your love,

Or don't allow me to speak to anyone!

Either keep me from paying attention to anything in the
world,

Or take me out of it.

O true Lord and my Glory!

How delicate yet extremely heavy

Is the cross you have prepared for those who reach this state!

Delicate because it's pleasing;

Heavy because at times one cannot bear it.

And yet, the soul would never want to be free of it

Except for the sake of being with you.

When it recalls that it hasn't served you in anything,

And that by living, it can still serve you,

It would want to carry a much heavier cross

And not die until the end of the world.

It finds no rest in anything,

Except offering you some small service.

It doesn't know what it wants,

But only understands it wants nothing other than you.

9

Ecstasy Is Not a Drug

"May the Lord give me the words to explain
something about the fourth water.
Clearly I need his favor, even more so than previously."

Put on your rain gear and get ready! According to Teresa this is where the soul gets saturated.

Teresa says, "In all the types of prayer that were explained, the gardener does some work, although in the latter degrees the work is accompanied by so much of God's glory and so many consolations that the soul would never want to abandon this prayer. As a result prayer isn't experienced as work, but rather, as glory.

"In this fourth kind of water for the garden, the soul isn't in possession of the senses, but it rejoices without knowing what it's rejoicing in. It realizes that it's enjoying something good, and this good encompasses all good together, but the good itself is incomprehensible. All the senses are occupied in this joy in a way that prevents them from being taken up by anything else."

Here we'll scarcely breathe. It will be hard to so much as wiggle a finger. Our senses will be rendered useless, so quiet that we'll lose all awareness of them. Teresa's friend St. John of the Cross wrote about this experience in his poem *The Dark Night of the Soul*:

> One dark night,
> fired with love's urgent longings
> —ah, the sheer grace—
> I went out unseen,
> my house being now all stilled.

The "house" John refers to as being stilled refers to the senses, but it also includes the faculties, passions, and sensual appetites. I know. We've been over all of this, but silencing of the faculties here is more intense and allows us to truly attend to being in God's embrace.

Don't worry. It's unlikely the family will find you in a vegetative state and call an ambulance. First of all, these states of suspended faculties are brief, so much so that beginners don't know they've experienced them. They only know that something wonderful has happened. Teresa, for example, never experienced this state for more than half an hour. I can't imagine it going on for that long.

The only time I can recall experiencing my senses being stilled happened a few times right after I took Communion. These were no long, drawn-out experiences. They were moments so fleeting I'm tempted to talk myself out of them. But I can't, because as I've suggested, they were transformative. In those sacred moments I felt as if my soul reached beyond all boundaries and kissed God. And he, in turn, kissed me.

When the Beloved kisses you it feels like your life, your whole being, is absorbed into that sacred kiss. Any sense of self as separate from this kiss vanishes. It's the difference between being in love and being love. Your senses can't process what is happening. Your mind can't. If bodies had fuse boxes, his kiss would blow every one of them.

I'd sit there on the pew or kneeler dumbstruck, possibly holding my breath, I really don't know. Tears I had no control over streamed down my cheeks. For a mere breath of time I was completely lost in God. Then I'd be aware again, a little disoriented as my body tried to catch up with my soul and completely mortified that I was crying when no one else was.

The Song of Songs has a verse Teresa loved about God's kiss: "Let him kiss me with the kisses of his mouth." It may sound a wee bit redundant, that whole "kisses of his mouth" thing, but hidden in those few words are a bit of exquisite wisdom. When we first come to God, we are like the sinful woman in Luke 7:36–39:

One of the Pharisees asked him over for a meal. He went to the Pharisee's house and sat down at the dinner table. Just then a woman of the village, the town harlot, having learned that Jesus was a guest in the home of the Pharisee, came with a bottle of very expensive perfume and stood at his feet, weeping, raining tears on his feet. Letting down her hair, she dried his feet, kissed them, and anointed them with the perfume. When the Pharisee who had invited him saw this, he said to himself, "If this man was the prophet I thought he was, he would have known what kind of woman this is who is falling all over him."

This is not the act of a proud woman. She was both humble and bold, and full of compunction. Bold because she crashed the party and swept past the stares and insults burning into her. Humble because she had not yet become God's friend and could only, in great sorrow, kiss his feet.

From there, a relationship begins. Remember how Christ showed Teresa his hands? In prayer, as we grow our friendship with the Lord, we can kiss his hands. Next Jesus showed Teresa his face, and afterward she could boldly say, "Let him kiss me with the kisses of his mouth." And that, my friends, is union. We don't dare ask until we have known Christ in the most basic, simple ways. We pray. We hear his voice in the Scriptures. We visualize him interiorly. We wait with him, and for him, until we are so fired with holy longing we lift our faces for his kiss.

We cannot attain this of our own. The Beloved only kisses his bride. He is a chaste groom, truer than true. But if you are fortunate enough to find yourself kissed by him, like Teresa, you may be swept off your feet. Literally.

Teresa was known to have extraordinary experiences in which she begged her nuns to hold her body down to keep her from levitating. Some say this was only a feeling, like vertigo, which waylaid her since her faculties, now suspended, were completely out of sorts. But stranger things are known to have happened, such as the prophet Elijah never tasting death, being whisked into eternity by an extraordinary, divine whirlwind of a favor.

Don't worry. I'm not going to go all woo-woo on you. (Or "mystical," if you prefer.) Most of us wouldn't want to levitate in prayer anyway. Teresa didn't. Strange phenomena embarrassed her. So, if you do want to levitate, it's probably for all the wrong reasons. Let's move on, shall we? The point I'm trying to make is that many of us long for an extraordinary love affair with one whose love is more intoxicating than wine.

You may be wondering how to know if you're on the right track to be kissed by God. Don't worry. Holy longing, an over-whelming, aching desire to be with your Beloved, will drive you to this level of intimacy. You will simply want to be in God's presence increasingly and crave more and more of him. Do try to enjoy the journey getting there. The weather on the top of that mountain is fair, the air clear, and it's plenty sunny. Teresa says, "The soul understands very well the sun's brightness and intensity, for it is powerful enough to melt the soul away."

That soul sunshine is God's dazzling presence, my friends, and the experience of faculty suspension is called ecstasy. It's not a drug. It's your personal experience of the miracle Jesus performed at the wedding in Cana. Having soaked your garden in rain, the Beloved turns the water into the finest wine, and you can drink to your fill.

You'll never wake up with a hangover. And be warned! It's highly addictive. I crave daily Communion because of just a little sprinkle of it. Right now I go twice a week to Mass, but holy longing makes this terribly unsatisfying. I'm working on upping the ante, pilgrims. Pray for me. Until then, I'll dream of more of this union.

In this state you really can spend hours at a time in prayer. Teresa tells us, "Once the faculties have begun to taste the divine wine and are drunk with it, they easily lose themselves again, in order to gain much more. All the faculties rejoice."

That pesky wild man will awaken, but who cares? While we're in this state we aren't worried about him! He's too incapacitated to do any real damage. Only those who've experienced it really know what it's like. The Lord told Teresa: "The soul detaches itself from everything, daughter, so it can abide more fully in me. It is no longer the soul that lives but I. Since it's not capable of comprehending what it understands, there is an understanding by not understanding."

Say what?

I told you it's hard to grasp these concepts if you haven't experienced them. Teresa says, "All I can say is the soul appears to be joined to God, and it's certain that this union has happened. In this prayer, the faculties fail, and are so suspended you can't tell they work. If you were meditating on Scripture, you don't remember what you were meditating on. If you were reading, you have no idea what you read, nor do you have any memory of vocal prayers you may have prayed. That annoying little moth that is the memory has its wings singed here. It can no longer move. The will is busy loving, but it doesn't understand how it loves. The intellect, if it can understand a thing, can't comprehend how it is comprehending. I can't understand this, myself!"

I'm beginning to see that, Teresa. Maybe it's as she suggested. This isn't an experience you think through. If I described what it's like to share an intimate kiss with my husband, it wouldn't do the amazing experience justice. My telling you about it isn't the same as you kissing my husband, deeply, yourself.

But hey, don't go deep-kissing my husband. My other Beloved is always available to romance you.

Sit with that awhile.

Teresa's Prayer

My Lord, the only thing I ask for in life
is that you kiss me with the kiss of your mouth,
and that you do so in such a way
that although I may want to withdraw
from this friendship and this union,
my will, Lord of my life, may always
be subject to your will
and never depart from it.
May nothing impede me
from being able to say: My God
and my glory, yes indeed
your breasts are better
and more delightful
than wine.

10

The Door to the Castle

"If you reflect carefully on this, my friends, you will see that the soul of the just person is like a paradise, where the Lord says he finds his delight. I have found nothing that compares to the magnificent beauty of a soul and its marvelous magnitude."

ood news, pilgrims! We won't be getting wet for a while. It's time to take off these drenched clothes and put on something a little more comfortable. You'll soon see what I mean, but for now, we're about to play. Hard. And we won't always play it safe in here.

We're going to enter and explore *The Interior Castle*, Teresa's most interesting and enduring book, written fourteen years after her autobiography. Here she's at her sassy best, more confident and powerful than ever. She's also more complex. Vibrant, sensual images illustrating the soul's journey to God abound. The exact same concepts she grappled with in her autobiography are explained with relative ease here, and in greater depth. But don't worry. Our focus will be a little different. There is one matter you shouldn't forget, however; we're going to be exploring mysteries. They can't be fully explained or understood.

That doesn't mean *The Interior Castle* is inaccessible. Teresa gives practical information as valuable to postmodern pilgrims as it was to her nuns in the sixteenth century. But the beauty of *The Interior Castle*—its real drawing power—is what it teaches about the soul.

Teresa says, "It came to me that the soul is like a castle made out of a single diamond, or a very clear crystal in which there are many rooms, just as in heaven there are many mansions."

That puts a whole new spin on Jesus' words, "In my Father's house there are many mansions." I can't help but pause at the breathtaking thought that the God who created all things—the mountains, the oceans, the Grand Canyon, the sky, and red velvet cake—would find my soul so beautiful that he wants the master suite inside of it. But Teresa is firm in her belief that it's true.

"Let's imagine," she says, "there are many rooms in this castle, some above; some below; others at either side; and in the center, amid them all, is the most important room of all, where God and the soul share the most sacred intimacies."

When she said many dwellings, she didn't mean a few dozen. Some of the dwellings have millions of rooms! The soul, after all, is big.

There's an outer wall to our soul, the castle—that's the body; and in Teresa's imagery, the five senses—seeing, hearing, smelling, tasting, touching—are like people inside. Our faculties are here, too—the intellect, will, imagination, and memory. They guard the castle—badly, Teresa would add—but they are its designated caretakers.

The question is, how do we get inside to the place where our Beloved waits to know us? I'll let our guide answer.

"My understanding is that the entry door to this castle is prayer. I'm not referring to prayer in the mind more than prayer on the lips, since in order for vocal prayer to be prayer at all it must be accompanied by reflection. If a person fails to consider who it is they're talking to, what they're asking for, or who they are that they dare to speak to God, I don't consider what they're doing as prayer, no matter how much they move their lips.

"Sometimes a person will be able to pray without this reflection, as long as a great deal of time has already been spent practicing prayer with reverence and awareness on other occasions. Talking to God like he's a slave, without being careful about how you approach him, and saying whatever comes to your head or relying on rote repetition is not praying in my opinion."

There Are Many Ways to Be in the Castle

I remember a time when I used to pray in a way that was a lot like me barking at God about who I was, and what he had promised for me. I had been taught how to pray this way, but it made me feel a little arrogant. God hadn't forgotten any of these things. He knew who I was, what he had said in Scripture, and what was best for me at every moment. I was praying in a way that had little to do with asking God that his will be done.

Lord, forgive me. I wasn't listening to my Beloved at all, nor did I leave much room to properly—and humbly—adore him. Even if all those words I said were true, praying like that made me feel entitled to God's blessings, rather than grateful for them. I've learned my lesson, friends. Thank God!

Central to Teresa's metaphor about the soul being a castle is the idea that we enter into it. If the castle is the soul, clearly you don't have to go inside of it, since it's pretty much you. Teresa wanted us to know something we shouldn't forget: "There are many ways to be inside the castle."

Still, some people stay just outside of it, in the outer courts where the guards stand. They don't care to go in at all, nor do they wish to know who lives inside in that most important suite full of delights. Neither do they wish to know what's in the rooms.

You'll also notice people hanging around the outer wall who are quite ill. These are souls who don't practice prayer at all. Teresa says, "They're like disabled people; even though they have hands and feet, they can't use them. These souls are so sick and accustomed to being absorbed by external matters that you can't help them, nor are they capable of going within themselves. Though by nature these souls are richly endowed with the power to speak with God himself, they're almost hopeless. If they don't take measures to understand themselves or the terrible danger they're in, they'll become like Lot's wife. She turned back to her old life and became a pillar of salt for her disobedience to God's instructions.

"Let's not keep our focus on these broken souls right now. They're like the man who waited thirty years beside the healing waters of Bethsaida. They're in a miserable, precarious state unless the Lord commands them to rise."

Right now, approaching the door of the castle, we're not in much of a position to help them. We're a bit engaged ourselves, which reminds me. There's something important I need to tell you.

Safety Precautions

We haven't talked about this much. I've wanted this journey to be fun, but a good friend doesn't put her companions in peril. I need to warn you about a few things before we approach the door of the castle.

We have an enemy who doesn't want us to go inside. In fact, if we find we have trouble seeing the big, beautiful mansion Teresa envisioned, it may be because this adversary shrouds the doorway in darkness. Or the darkness could be because of our own failure to look at ourselves. The devil benefits from this kind of ignorance. But God is merciful. He's given us a few tools to shatter that darkness.

This would be a good time to put the armor of God on over your everyday clothes. Yes, it's the same one you learned about in Sunday school. Maybe you had one of those cute little "whole armor of God" superhero costumes sold at Christian bookstores. Or maybe you have no idea what I'm talking about. Paul speaks of it in Ephesians 6:10–18:

> God is strong, and he wants you strong. So take everything the Master has set out for you, well-made weapons of the best materials. And put them to use so you will be able to stand up to everything the Devil throws your way. This is no afternoon athletic contest that we'll walk away from and forget about in a couple of hours. This is for keeps, a life-or-death fight to the finish against the Devil and all his angels.
>
> Be prepared. You're up against far more than you can handle on your own. Take all the help you can get, every weapon God has issued, so that when it's all over but the shouting you'll still be on your feet. Truth, righteousness, peace, faith, and salvation are more than words. Learn how to apply them. You'll need them throughout your life. God's Word is an indispensable weapon. In the same way, prayer is essential in this ongoing warfare. Pray hard and long. Pray for your brothers and sisters. Keep your eyes open. Keep each other's spirits up so that no one falls behind or drops out.

We must be diligent. Our enemy is tricky. He's been around a lot longer than we have and is adept at deception. The old church mothers used to tell me, "The devil is a liar, and there ain't no truth in him." Nothing made that fact clearer to me than when, a few years ago, just before I was due to attend one of my favorite spirituality conferences, I was besieged by a flurry of thoughts that insisted that I was a whore.

Yes, I said the "w" word, because that is exactly what my soul's enemy said, which was way harsh. I have to admit I have a few things in common with those reformed harlots of the desert whose conversion stories move me so. But not that much! At the time of this attack I was married, the mother of a small tribe, and suffering from acute fibromyalgia syndrome, while I struggled to write Christian fiction. I rarely got out of the house long enough to catch a glimpse of a man, much less proposition any. The whole idea was ludicrous, but I did little to defend myself against this painful assault, simply because I'd violated the virtue of chastity in my past. God had forgiven me, but I hadn't forgiven myself. The enemy pounced on my guilt and magnified it completely out of proportion. He did the same to Jesus. Take a look at Matthew, chapter 4: "Next Jesus was taken into the wild by the Spirit for the Test. The Devil was ready to give it. Jesus prepared for the test by fasting forty days and forty nights. That left him, of course, in a state of extreme hunger, which the Devil took advantage of in the first test: 'Since you are God's Son, speak the word that will turn these stones into loaves of bread.'"

Turning stones to bread is a far cry from simply tempting Jesus to break his fast, especially since Jesus was already famished! But that's our enemy's modus operandi. *The Message* explains: "Jesus answered by quoting Deuteronomy: 'It takes more than bread to stay alive. It takes a steady stream of words from God's mouth.'"

Another temptation followed, and Jesus wielded the sword of the Word once again. This time he used a quote from Psalm 91. But alas, the devil is nothing if not persistent. He came back with one more temptation before Jesus gave him a final smack down: "'Beat it, Satan!' He backed his rebuke with a third quotation from Deuteronomy: 'Worship the Lord your God, and only him. Serve him with absolute single-heartedness.'"

If Jesus used spiritual weapons to fight spiritual battles, how dare we not fortify ourselves with such vital armor?

There's another thing. Once we're closer to the doorway of the castle, you're going to have to watch your step! There are all kinds of reptiles, lizards, and poisonous vipers on the ground. Those are our worldly attachments. Everything we desire of the world is there: power, influence, affluence, lust, ambition, and a host of other temptations. One of my snakes is vanity. I don't care how much of a ragamuffin I say I am, I'm inordinately attached to wanting to look pretty. Vanity often comes with its companion, reckless fear-driven spending. The slippery little beast lives to make my vanity happy.

When I was a little girl I used to be afraid of the earthworms that heavy rainstorms washed onto the sidewalks. Sometimes I closed my eyes and tried to run to school. I must admit, running on wet pavement with my eyes shut when I'm inherently clumsy is a colossally bad idea. I'll spare you the details. Suffice it to say that we can't ignore the snakes and reptiles in our path and hope we make it to the castle despite ourselves. No, we'll have to pray our way past these beasts, using all the methods we know to work. Then we'll be in! Although I'm sure Teresa would toss this caveat our way to keep us humble: "We have done very well to have gotten in at all." Ain't that the truth?

Trust Your Journey

11

Dwellings One, Two, and Three

*"It is very important for a soul who practices prayer,
no matter how little or much, to explore these dwelling places
without holding back. Don't stay in one corner.
Go up above, down below, and to the sides,
because God has given it such resplendent dignity."*

W e need to talk. I know a few of you may think that when a woman says, "We need to talk," there's going to be trouble, and I'm sorry to say that this time—it's true. Remember when I said we were going to reimagine the word "saint"? Well, there's another troubling word that starts with the letter "s," and we have to look at it just the way it is. Pilgrims, it's time to talk seriously about *sin*.

Before I take Communion I pray, "Lord, I am not worthy to receive you, but only say the word and I shall be healed." Often in my private devotions I pray like our Eastern Orthodox

Christian brothers and sisters do daily, saying, "Lord, have mercy." This is a short version of the classic Jesus prayer, "Lord Jesus Christ, Son of the living God, have mercy on me, a sinner." I need these prayers.

When I was a rabid fundamentalist I rarely thought of myself as a sinner. Sometimes I succeeded in deceiving myself into believing the list of things I didn't do made me righteous; but I wasn't righteous. And you need to decide if you are. We need to be aware of our propensity to do wrong; otherwise we're doomed to continue in sin.

I can't emphasize enough what an affront our gross sins are to our Beloved. We all have petty faults and our diligent practice of prayer safeguards us from these. But some of us have big-ticket-item sins, the kind the Catholic Church calls "mortal" sins. That's not fancy terminology that applies only to Catholics. Mortal sins are the deeds we do—or don't do—that put our souls in grave danger. They aren't "mistakes." These are quite deliberate. You do them with full knowledge and consent. The Ten Commandments enumerates mortal sins, but those are just some big 'uns. At the risk of making some of you very uncomfortable, I'm going to share what some of the other sins are that the Bible behooves us to flee. Paul gives us the short list in Galatians 5:19–20:

> It is obvious what kind of life develops out of trying to get your own way all the time: repetitive, loveless, cheap sex; a stinking accumulation of mental and emotional garbage;

frenzied and joyless grabs for happiness; trinket gods; magic-show religion; paranoid loneliness; cutthroat competition; all-consuming-yet-never-satisfied wants; a brutal temper; an impotence to love or be loved; divided homes and divided lives; small-minded and lopsided pursuits; the vicious habit of depersonalizing everyone into a rival; uncontrolled and uncontrollable addictions; ugly parodies of community. I could go on.

This isn't the first time I have warned you, you know. If you use your freedom this way, you will not inherit God's kingdom.

You should be doing some business with God now.

Teresa advises, "Before I go on you should consider what would happen to this luminous beautiful castle, this pearl of the East, this tree of life planted in the living waters of life itself, if the soul were to fall into mortal sin. There's no darker night, or blackness more obscuring. Although the same sun that gives the soul such brilliance and beauty remains in the center, the soul is no longer able to experience its light. Yet, it's still as capable of enjoying His Majesty as a crystal is capable of reflecting the sun's brilliance. Nothing helps a soul in this condition, and as a result, all the good works it does while in this state profit it nothing.

"They cannot be pleasing in God's sight. Since it's the intention of anyone who commits these sins to please the devil who is darkness itself, instead of God, the poor soul also becomes darkness itself."

Teresa explains that we are essentially separated from God when we're in grave sin. I also believe we're simply too proud to admit our failures. Never forget that pride was the sin that got Satan cast out of heaven with a host of angels. He was too vain to realize that no, he was not equal to God. Oh, if so many self-righteous postmodern Pharisees in our churches today were brave enough to say the same: "I am not equal to God." Imagine what that kind of humility would do.

I interrupt this chapter for an important message from our sponsor:

An Impassioned Plea from Teresa

O souls
set free by the blood of Jesus Christ!
Learn to understand and have compassion for
    yourselves.
Strive to lift the black cloak that darkens the crystal of
    your soul.
If your life were to end right now in such a perilous state
you would never enjoy this light again.
O Jesus! It's a sad thing to see a soul separated from this
    light.

What's the point of a prayer pilgrimage if our actions separate us from God? I urge you, try not to offend the Beloved. We'll find ourselves uncomfortable in our own soul's home. That's no way to live.

. . .

Now it's time to turn our attention to the first dwelling in this marvelous castle. Do you notice it's rather dark in here? That's because the light I told you about doesn't seem to reach these first few chambers. These rooms are not black, like rooms are when the soul is darkened by grave sin. It's just that those pesky snakes and reptiles—the ones that followed us in—are doing their job keeping your soul from perceiving its radiance.

It's like having mud in your eyes. You can hardly open them to see. But the little beast slithering around your feet that came through the door with you may capture your attention.

Teresa says, "Even though a soul may not be in a terrible state, it's so busy with worldly things and absorbed by its possessions, honors, and business affairs that even if it did want to see the beauty of the dwelling, those things won't allow it to."

I know she was talking to nuns, but this applies to us, too. She says, "Each one should do what's in their power to do, according to their lifestyle. This is so important if you're going to reach the main dwelling place. It's so vital that I doubt you'll get there without this kind of comittment. And it will be impossible to stay where you are without danger even though you're in the castle, because if you're standing in the middle of a bunch of poisonous creatures, you're bound to get bit!"

This is where self-knowledge comes in handy. Your castle has millions of rooms, and the room of self-knowledge is huge. Go back there often, and do, my friends, go with God. Return to

your exercises such as a daily examen, as well as journaling. Take
a mega supply of humility with you. You're going to need it when
you get busy about the pride-busting task of facing yourself.

I hate to bring him up again, but Teresa warned of something else in the first dwelling. "There are many people who,
because of their sins, fall back into misery. In a monastery
you're free from outside concerns to focus on spiritual matters. There are very few dwelling places in our castle in which
devils can't bother us. In some rooms the guards—our faculties, working together with our senses—have grown strong
enough to fight. But we can't grow lax in recognizing the wiles
of the devil. He's tricky enough to change himself into an angel of light. Little by little, he can do us harm if we don't rec-
ognize him for who he is."

Teresa gives us some ridiculously thinly veiled examples from
her own life. She'd been zealous enough to demand perfection
from herself and was only at rest when she was beating herself
mercilessly for the slightest imperfection. Keep in mind: she
did live in the sixteenth century. Zeal for right living is good,
but not if you're so hard on yourself that you make yourself
sick. And be careful not to fall into finding easy fault with other
people, magnifying their imperfections. The devil loves it when
our love cools for others.

I'm ashamed to admit that at my most self-righteous times
I've expressed alleged "concerns" about people whom I knew were
struggling with sin. I went about assassinating the characters of
these poor souls under the guise of sharing their needs so I

could pray about them with others. Lord, have mercy. What's worse is that I had little insight into my cruelty.

Jesus taught that true perfection means loving God and loving our neighbor. I don't care how good it looks, if anything you experience in your castle doesn't urge you toward loving God and your neighbor, tell it to "get thee behind me." Or if you like to shake things up a bit, "Satan, get lost. You have no idea how God works" (Matthew 16:23).

We have to be wise as the serpents nipping our heels and harmless as doves. Only then can we move forward.

THE SECOND DWELLING

Hellooooo . . . . ? Can you hear me? It's awfully noisy in here, and there are still a lot of devils, snakes, and reptiles to fight. We're closer to the Beloved. The intellect has grown sharper here, and the faculties more skillful. It's pretty explosive, pilgrims, so watch your backs!

Something shifts inside. Now demons actively engage the serpents and reptiles. Suddenly our worldly pleasures and attachments seem so much more important. Diseases of the soul such as affluenza can sicken us so badly that, if we're not careful, all our wanting stuff will cost us the strength to persevere. And that's just one example.

The lure of the world is strong. Ambition is lauded by most. Few people are going to use the Beatitudes as a formula for success. Blessed are the poor in spirit? Sure, as long as it doesn't interfere with us having a really nice car and other comforts.

And sin still nags us. Lust of the flesh surges through our bodies as sex, sex, sex bombards us in the media. Humans are sexual beings. How we respond to this onslaught, how much importance these things take on in our lives, will determine whether or not we make it through these rooms of Teresa's metaphorical castle.

One of Teresa's struggles, stemming from her childhood, was her cavernous need for approval. I, a person who was not raised by either of my parents, have the same obsession. Somewhere deep inside, I'm always trying to right the notion that there is something wrong with me, and I have to charm, delight, or manipulate people so that they'll love me. It's hard to shake this viper, and I get discouraged when I fail so often.

Teresa suggests enlisting the caretakers and guards of the castle—our faculties and senses—to come to our aid. She says, "Reason shows us that the soul is mistaken if it thinks the things of the world are more important that what it's pursuing. But faith teaches it about where it can find true fulfillment. Memory helps it to see how fleeting life is, and how even the rich die suddenly; their riches can't keep the living from walking over their graves. The soul itself can consider these matters, and other hard things."

But our practice of prayer changes our perception. Spending time with God begets love of God, and our faculties yield to love.

"The will is inclined to love after seeing countless signs of love; it would want to love God in return, especially if it understands its true Lover never leaves it and accompanies it, giving it life and being. The intellect is enlisted in convincing the soul that it could find no better friend than this Lover, even if it lived many years. The world is full of falsehood, and the pleasures of sin come with trials, cares, and contradictions. The intellect also tells the soul that outside of the castle it will find no peace, so it should avoid going to strange houses since its own home is filled with blessings."

These are strong statements for the postmodern believer to hear, and I realize they may sound a little foreign. Perhaps it's easy to trust the simple words of Jesus in Matthew 6:21: "The place where your treasure is, is the place you will most want to be, and end up being."

So, what does it mean to be in this castle? Why did Teresa create this elaborate metaphor for our Christian lives? Here Teresa draws upon her love for chivalrous tales by trading the image of the master gardener for the lofty depiction of a great and powerful king. The soul is where the Lord, the King of kings, finds his delight, and nothing is more magnificent, immense, or noble than his castle. Teresa's vision of the soul is more mature now, and her confidence more robust. I believe by the time she wrote *The Interior Castle*, she was far more at peace with mystery. She knew her readers could never truly fathom that we are made in the image and likeness of God, and it is equally as difficult to dare to believe our souls possess such beauty and amplitude. Oh, but for our own sakes we must try to believe it, and she gave all she had to convince us of this important truth.

Through the interior castle, Teresa urges us to know ourselves and the nature of our souls. If we don't, how can we possibly understand the treasures housed within us, including its powerful, yet compassionate occupant, the King of kings? Most of us waste our energy focusing on the outer wall—our bodies—instead of meandering through the countless rooms in our castle. Teresa's challenge for us is to move beyond the superficial and explore our vast, spectacular inner edifices.

The Third Dwelling

Teresa knew how difficult the first two rooms would be with so many enemies. We don't dare relax and take our armor off or put our weapons down. What if our enemies find us weak and give us a beat-down?

But when we understand that the soul is like a castle, and there are rooms in which we have the ability to fight for our spiritual lives—with the King of kings on our side—we begin to see what a powerful journey this can be.

In the third dwelling of this castle that is our soul, we realize our diligence in the first two dwellings has paid off. We've been behaving ourselves for quite some time now. Perhaps we're feeling so comfortable that we're actually teaching others what we know about the castle. We can't get too comfortable, however, because His Majesty himself has been known to send a few tests our way here. They won't be tests to see if we are loyal. We've proven we have what it takes to stay the course. That doesn't mean we're without the nagging little sins we're all prone to. It means we try hard not to cause any offense to the King. But we aren't quite where we think we are. When we react out of proportion to tests of will and challenges, such as by complaining incessantly that we don't deserve the difficulties we're confronted with, we prove we still have a way to go in growing to adulthood.

We who may consider ourselves to be God's most trusted, devoted servants could very well find the door to the Beloved's honeymoon suite closed to us, and boy, are we gonna be mad about it! But closed doors can be a challenge. How badly do we want to enter into this chamber where God's deepest secrets are whispered in our ears?

Consider the story of the prodigal son's brother. He got a little salty with his dad when the guy who messed up all the time and came back home dragging his knuckles on the ground and smelling like swine got the roast, the robe, the ring, and the rockin' party. Or think of the wealthy young man in the Gospel of Luke (18:18–23), who had this remarkable encounter with Jesus:

> One day one of the local officials asked him, "Good Teacher, what must I do to deserve eternal life?"
>
> Jesus said, "Why are you calling me good? No one is good—only God. You know the commandments, don't you? No illicit sex, no killing, no stealing, no lying, honor your father and mother."
>
> He said, "I've kept them all for as long as I can remember."
>
> When Jesus heard that, he said, "Then there's only one thing left to do: Sell everything you own and give it away to the poor.

You will have riches in heaven. Then come, follow me."

This was the last thing the official expected to hear. He was very rich and became terribly sad. He was holding on tight to a lot of things and not about to let them go.

This is the work of the third dwelling: Are we willing to be mature enough to relinquish our attachments, even the ones that seem oh-so-spiritual, which still hold so much power in our lives? Pilgrims, will we walk away from Jesus sad, having given little of what he really wants from us?

Keep praying your way through the castle, come what may. Be content to be God's servant, ever ready to do as he asks you. Try not to expect more than you're entitled to, or you might end up like the prodigal son's brother, angry and bitter, even though you, too, are a beloved son. Stay humble.

Now, take my hand. Things are about to get interesting.

12

The Fourth Dwelling

"Since these dwelling places are closer to where the King lives, their beauty is majestic. There are things to see and understand so exquisite that the intellect lacks the words to explain them."

In the previous two chapters, we entered Teresa's metaphor of the Interior Castle—the first three dwellings:

- In the first, it's hard to get past the snakes and reptiles, but If we make it inside we're at least warring with ourselves and our enemy.
- In the second, we deal with our sins and visit the room of self-knowledge often, as we gain humility. The lure of the world is still strong.
- In the third dwelling we may have become upstanding, deeply spiritual people who do not wish to offend God at all, but we are still immature and can complain and fold under the weight of tests we may think we don't deserve to go through.

- Hence, we need *more* humility and perseverance.
- We're challenged to surrender all to be with the Beloved, like the rich young man in Luke, chapter 18.
- It can take many years to get through these three dwellings. They parallel the first few stages of watering the garden.

Now, don't get too comfortable in these first three rooms, because if you're wise, you won't spend a lot of time in this part of the castle. That doesn't mean it isn't an awesome place to be. Teresa is grinning now as she guides us into the fourth dwelling. It's prettier here; the room is well lit. It takes most people a long time to get here, but that's not a rule. Some will make it here relatively fast. That is up to them and the Beloved. However long it took you to get here, enjoy it.

Take heart—looking around, I don't see a single poisonous creature. I'm sure one or two are lurking, but they're harmless, actually doing us some good. Teresa tells us, "Without temptation, the devil could deceive us regarding spiritual consolations and thereby hurt us much more. And our souls would benefit far less if every opportunity for gaining spiritual rewards were withdrawn and we were completely absorbed in God. If a soul is in one continuous state it's not safe—not while we're in exile. Nor do I think it's possible to for the Spirit of the Lord to be fixed in one place in this world."

But don't worry yourself about those matters. You are quite close to goodness beyond measure. So you must attend to your soul and mind your behavior; things are going to move more quickly now. Imagine how Teresa's eyes must be bright with holy mischief as she guides us now, because we're about to enter the realm of the supernatural.

What? You thought we'd already gone there when we were fighting all those demons? Well, sure we did, but Teresa is about to take us deeper into the heart of God. This part isn't about our enemy! We're so much closer to the King of kings' chamber.

In chapter five we touched upon the aridity we face in transitional periods when we grow from one degree of prayer to another, and in the previous two chapters we talked about crosses we bear and disappointments we face in the spiritual life when Christ expects us to mature. Both these are times in which we may crave consolations. These are the warm feelings we receive in prayer that are so encouraging. But we can't be overly attached to them. Teresa had a lot to say about these matters when she talked about the fourth dwelling, and the differences between consolations and spiritual sweetness. They're important to understand, because here our holy longing grows increasingly more acute. We'll need to be prepared to go where this room will ultimately lead us.

"Consolations are those experiences that we ourselves acquire through our own prayers to the Lord. They proceed from our natures, although God has a hand in them, for it must be understood in whatever I say that without him I can do nothing. But consolations arise from the good works we do, and it seems like we've earned them through our diligent efforts, so we're rightly consoled. But if we think about this, we may find we experience the same consolations for many earthly things."

It's like being at the well with our shiny little buckets again. We feel good about the things we've done because we did them! But what if we hit the lottery? We're going to have several million consolations that feel pretty darned good. What about falling in love? It's glorious! And if a loved one is snatched back from the jaws of death? Oh, happy day! A well-lived life can overflow with consolations—and these are mostly earthly things. We're headed somewhere else.

Teresa doesn't mean that these consolations are bad. What she wants us to focus on is the fact that the good feelings come from us, but they end in God. Not so with spiritual sweetness and delight.

"Spiritual sweetness begins in God, and our human natures enjoy these delights just as much as the other kind I mentioned—even more, in fact, than the consolations I described.

"O Jesus, how I wish I knew how to explain this! I see the difference, but I don't have the ability to make it clear to my friends. Please help me teach them, Lord. Now I remember a line that we say when praying the hours at Prime. It's found in the last part of the verse at the end of the last psalm: *Cum dilatasti cor meum*—you have dilated my heart. . . ."

What a striking image that brings to mind: God gently taking our hearts and opening them by the warmth of his love. Teresa is beginning to share with us how, when we have come deep enough into the castle, by prayer, to be still with our God, we find sweetness and joy. This is a little piece of heaven right where we are.

To illustrate the delights of spiritual sweetness, Teresa allows us once again to play with water—a bountiful image for our guide, just as it was for the psalmists. She invites us, basin in hands, to stand by two fountains. You stand by one. I'll stand by the other. Let's listen:

"The two fountains fill with water in different ways. The water from one comes from far away and is channeled through many aqueducts employing a great deal of ingenuity."

That would be my fountain, the complicated noisy one.

And yours?

"For the other one the source of water is right there, and the basin fills noiselessly. If the spring is abundant, the water overflows and fills the basin. No skill is necessary, and you don't have to bother with aqueducts because water will always flow from the spring."

You're having a grand old time splashing around over there, aren't you? Can we get focused here? Although I think we know which one of the fountains is spiritual sweetness.

Teresa sits us down, wet clothes and all, and teaches us:

"I think the water that fills the first fountain, which comes from the aqueducts, is comparable to the consolations I mentioned that are drawn through our prayer efforts. We gain it by our thoughts, by meditating on created things, through our own efforts. A lot of commotion is made as the basin fills, but in the end, it certainly profits our souls.

"But the other fountain, the one that springs from God, is different. When His Majesty wants to bestow on us supernatural favors, the experience brings with it the greatest peace, quietude, and sweetness to our innermost depths of our being. I have no idea where it comes from or how it comes.

"This joy isn't like earthly pleasures that are felt by the heart, at least not at first. After gradually filling the soul to the brim, it overflows into all the faculties and each of the dwellings until it reaches the body. This is why I say it begins in God and ends in ourselves, because everyone who experiences it will see that every part of us, including our physical selves, shares in the delight and sweetness. This joy seems to originate not in our hearts, but some deeper part of our inner being."

If you think of this expansion as coming from the Beloved, there's no need to try to force anything to happen. Remember we talked about not wrestling our thoughts into submission? We can also rest in this fourth dwelling of the castle. God is here.

● ● ●

St. Teresa's Top Five Reasons to Cease Striving

1. We must love God above all and not allow self-interest to motivate us.

2. Our services to God are really insignificant. Thinking we're entitled to blessings is an affront to the virtue of humility.

3. The real preparation for these special gifts of sweetness comes not from desiring consolations but in our desire and willingness to suffer as our Beloved suffered.

4. While His Highness will surely grant us glory if we keep his commandments, he is not obligated to do us any favors just because we crave them. We can still be set free without our every whim being satisfied. God is God. He knows better than we do what's right for us.

5. And finally, striving for spiritual sweetness is a waste of time. This is not the water you carry yourself. It doesn't matter how much we pray or how many tears we shed, this kind of gift can't be manipulated. God gives it to whomever he wants to give it to, often when the soul least expects it. In any case, do pray no matter what!

This fourth room is decorated for a party. Twinkling strands of white lights lend a festive air to the already brilliantly lit room. We remain so very ordinary, yet the numinous mingles with the mundane of our lives. God is close enough for us to catch his scent. Through prayer we draw closer to the flame of divine love and feel its fire warming us. We are changing, just as Moses did when he had a supernatural encounter with the Lord on Mount Sinai. His face grew radiant. Why? Because he had been speaking with God.

Things happen when we talk to God. Trust him for everything your soul desires. Teresa's wisdom is our guide: "We belong to God, my friends. Let him do whatever he wants with us, and bring us wherever pleases him. I truly hope that if you humble yourself and stay detached—in other words, you aren't just thinking of being humble and detaching yourself, because your thoughts can deceive you—God will give you the favor of this sweet water and a multitude of blessing you don't know how to desire. May he be praised and blessed forever. Amen."

St. Teresa's Prayer

O my Lord and my God!
How great is your grandeur!
We walk about here below
Like foolish little shepherds,
Thinking we are gaining
Some knowledge of you,
But it amounts to nothing at all.

There are secrets within ourselves
We do not understand.
They don't compare to the secrets
Inside of you.
Your grandeur is extraordinary,
And our secrets, nothing at all.

13

The Mysteries of the
Bridal Chamber

*"If we gained nothing else in this way of prayer except to
understand the astonishing care God has in communing with us,
and his imploring us to remain in him—for that's exactly what
this experience is—it seems to me that all the trials endured for
the sake of enjoying those tender touches of his love, so sublime
and penetrating, would be worthwhile."*

SPIRITUAL
ADVISORY
MYSTERIOUS CONTENT

W
e need to talk again. Seriously. This isn't kid's stuff. Maybe it's time to put on more formal clothes. Why don't you try one of these nice white garments prepared for you? I think it's time. And may I say, you clean up real nice.

The content in this chapter is going to be more explicit and the mysteries more profound. This isn't spiritual milk, pilgrims, appropriate for babies. And it's not just any old steak you can pick up at the grocery store. We're about to consume *steak tartare*; it's raw, and a little dangerous. You can only get this at the grown folks' table.

To help you understand these next few dwellings, I'm going to share a Scripture passage with you that is pregnant with the kind of mystery I'm alluding to.

In Ephesians 5:29–32, the apostle Paul offered a startling metaphor that has disturbed many a pilgrim. But we're going to be brave. I'm not even going to quote it from *The Message* this time. This Scripture shakes *me* up a bit. "For no man ever hates his own flesh, but nourishes it, and cherishes it, as Christ does the church, because we are members of His body. For this reason, a man shall leave his father and mother and be joined to his wife, and the two shall become one flesh. This mystery is a profound one, and I'm saying it refers to Christ and the church" (RSV).

Heady stuff, isn't it?

To give you a little context of the culture that formed Paul's bold statement, I'm going to tell you a bit about ancient Jewish wedding customs.

Th
betro
famil
and t
No
exclu
the c
is pro
On
groo
wher
of sep
herse
Me
he re
groo
prisin
shout
At l
rejoic
father
Sho
the w
accon
until
consu
guest

bridal chamber. There as the place where
seven days of the wed e are given the gift
Perhaps you recogni —the peace-infused
ing parables of Jesus. I ver of quiet." Psalm
return for us. It points this experience.
mystery of intimacy be
you, and Christ and m
Many men may have
Steve told me, not su
being the Bride of Ch
a guy that Jesus coul
shoulder hugs to. Still
as lover, too. It was T
opened himself to thee, a precious pearl of
from his *Spiritual Can* us prepare our souls
re to us." Ah, but we
In the inner wine ce nake the difference.
I drank of my Belov wants everything for
through all this valle have given, you will
I no longer knew an
and lost the herd tha lly grasp this, Teresa
There he gave me h
there he taught me a elous way that silk is
and I gave myself to something like this.
keeping nothing bac ize of tiny grains of
and the leaves on the
to nourish themselves

on mulberry leaves until they grow to full size. That's when they settle on to some twigs and go about spinning the silk with their tiny mouths, until they make the narrow, silken cocoons they burrow in. Soon our plump and homely worm dies, and a graceful white butterfly is born and flies away."

Our souls are those little life seeds, and according to Teresa the heat of the Holy Spirit quickens us and we come alive. The things God brings our way to help us in the spiritual life are what nourish us: confession, reading good books, and hearing inspiring sermons. These things sustain us, along with our practice of prayer and reflection, until we grow into mature grubby little worms and build the silken house around us that we will die in.

Christ is our cocoon. Colossians 3:3 confirms, "For you have died, and your life is hid with Christ in God" (RSV). We don't cease to exist here. We are transformed into new, more beautiful creatures.

"Courage, my friends," Teresa admonishes us. "Let's be quick to do this work and weave our little cocoons by getting rid of our self-centeredness, willfulness, and attachments to earthly things, and by performing acts of penance, prayer, self-denial, obedience, and all the other things you already know how to do."

Isn't it strange how we cling to the idea that there's some elusive prayer formula that will revolutionize our devotional lives, if only we could figure it out? And of course, we can't figure it out. We rarely trust what we already know how to do, which is why we miss many precious encounters with God. All we need to master prayer is a simple, loving relationship with our Beloved and friend. And what do you do when you're with your friends? Probably the stuff you always do together.

My friend Evette's favorite color is purple. I know the name of the man who broke her heart, but I could also tell you about the myriad small things—and people—that mend that generous heart back together.

My friend Lisa loves asparagus, and she doesn't like to get in trouble. Once upon a time she thought she was God's scullery maid, but now she's his love bug.

Mary hears words as if they're music. She has healing in her outrageous sense of humor. She longs for the return of her jewel of great price. These things I know.

I've spent time with these women. I love them, and have given myself to them, and receive an abundant bounty for having them in my life. Whatever I was before I met them, I'm not anymore, because they've all changed me.

So it is with God and in prayer, even more so. I know a few things about God because I've been with him: in church and out of it, in obedience, and in great remorse for my sins. I've known him as rescuer and afflicter, as giver and the one who loves me enough to take what I don't need away. I've felt him brood over me like the Holy Spirit brooded over the waters in Creation, and in the space of a breath I've known my Beloved's embrace, and for a moment he completely absorbed my being within himself. This closeness wounds me, but the agony is magnificent. Sometimes his wounds leave me baffled, unsure of who I am, or what I am; I only know I belong to him.

I used to work for an afterschool program. One spring we bought a butterfly kit to watch their metamorphosis from the larval stage. I didn't find caterpillars to be the most riveting creatures ever, but what fascinated me was when one of the butterflies finally emerged from its chrysalis. The process looked almost painful and was slower than I thought it would be. It didn't just break out of its enclosure like a baby chick pokes its way out of an egg. But when it had come through it, I noticed its wings were covered with a substance that looked suspiciously like blood. It perched on the mesh butterfly pavilion slowly flapping those red-streaked wings. The image haunted me.

I couldn't help but think of the spiritual life and how part of our metamorphosis is through suffering. We may be born anew in transformation, but our white wings are stained with blood, and thus we fly into our next stop.

THE SIXTH DWELLING

If holy longing begins in the fifth dwelling, it's heightened in the sixth until it's nearly unbearable. That's what Teresa tells us. The soul is wounded with love. The thought of offending His Majesty appalls it. Sin separates us from God, and here the soul can't abide any obstacles that will stand between it and the Beloved. Imagine the soul is now betrothed to Christ according to our model. She's caught a glimpse of him, and she's spent time with him, and now she recognizes he is perfection.

And he wants her. Her bride price was expensive, but he willingly paid it, and now she longs for the wait to be over so she can enter the bridal chamber and experience the fullness of his love.

I know some of you find such erotically charged imagery uncomfortable, perhaps especially some pilgrims of the male gender. Teresa recognized this, too. She said, "The comparison may be crude, but I can't think of a better one to explain the espousal of God and the soul than the sacrament of marriage. Spiritual espousal is different from the marriage between a man and woman because we're only dealing with spiritual things. The pleasures of the body a married couple experiences have nothing to do with the union of God and the soul; the delights the Lord gives the soul by comparison are a thousand miles distant. It's a matter of love united with love, and the acts of love are pure and exquisitely delicate, so gentle they can't be explained. But the Lord knows how to make you feel them." Oh, how we'll feel them, deep in the core of our being.

"The soul's rendezvous with her Beloved has left such an impression that her singular desire is to enjoy him again. Remember, nothing can be seen in this state of prayer, at least not in the ordinary sense of seeing. We can't even see this in our imaginations."

To be in this part of the castle is to never want to leave—to grow in love for God and, as we do, to remove other loves from our lives. "Now the soul is fiercely determined to take no other spouse but him. But the Beloved doesn't give in to her desire for a quickie marriage. He wants her to want him more and for their espousal to cost her something, since it's so precious a gift. And although whatever price must be paid for such immense blessings is little by comparison, she longs for a token that promises he will indeed join himself to her.

"This hope of espousal is necessary for us to endure the crosses we'll bear to get to the seventh dwelling," Teresa warns. Other suffering abounds, as well. Pilgrim spouses of Christ, when you are this deep into the castle's rooms, you'll meet the haters, those who will persecute you for righteousness's sake. They have no idea your friendship with God runs so deep, and some will accuse you mercilessly. My sister Carly once testified of her love for God and called him her "husband" during a service at her church. You'd have thought she said God was dead by the reaction she got from some of the people in the congregation. They insisted such familiarity with God was impossible, and the whole idea was offensive and extrabiblical. And weird. Perhaps they hadn't read Isaiah 54:5, which says, "For the Maker is your husband, the LORD of hosts is His name" (RSV), but Carly knew whom she belonged to and exactly who he was to her.

Praise is an even greater trial. This deep into the castle and you'll hardly be able to stand it. You know that even in this stage, so close to the bridal chamber, you can still be deceived by Satan and turn away from the graces so lavishly bestowed on you. Our guide teaches us, "We must be diligent, continuously praying that God will sustain us. If he abandons us, we'll fall into the abyss. We could never trust ourselves. That would be foolish. We should walk carefully, paying attention to how we practice virtue and whether we're becoming better or worse in some areas, especially loving one another, desiring to be least among our friends, and in performing well our ordinary tasks."

Other great trials will come our way. One of mine was chronic pain. It didn't just afflict my body; it wounded my soul. A few years ago, I found myself confined to bed so much I feared I'd soon have to go into a nursing home. I didn't dare believe I'd live to be fifty. The pain and fatigue stole a lot of life from me. That year I couldn't tell you the names of my children's schoolteachers. I never attended a parent-teacher conference, and my quality time with my babies consisted of them crawling in bed with me. Most days they couldn't hug me because my skin hurt to the touch.

I begged God to heal me, felt angry when he didn't grant my request, and grieved what felt like my own slow death. Sometimes I wrestled with God so violently, like Jacob, that I ended up with a limp.

My friend Terry prayed for my healing during this time, and the Lord told her, "I have Mair in my hands." His response puzzled both of us. I began to soften my heart to my illness and offer up my suffering as a sacrifice. Strange things began to happen after that.

One night I dreamed I bore two passion wounds of Christ, in my hands. When I awakened, a profound sense of God-infused peace covered me, which felt as luxurious as a velvet cloak. It wasn't just a dream. I'd had a visitation, and somehow I knew

God was not finished with my story. He was in my suffering; he willed it for some reason I couldn't understand, and still don't, but I trust him. Most days. God has met me in my bed of affliction. If I didn't have fibromyalgia, he and I would not be as friendly as we are.

There are other sufferings that we endure in this dwelling—interior ones, which even Teresa has trouble describing. But they are in short the same kind of arrow of love the angel plunged into Teresa. She says, "I know this pain seems to pierce the very heart, and when he who wounds it draws out the dart, it seems to pull the heart out with it, too, the love the soul feels is so deep."

All of these trials allow the little white butterfly to soar higher. Be they persecutions, dark nights of no consolations, physical illnesses, or the wounds of love, an assurance is found here that the woman in the Song of Songs knew: you are your Beloved's, and his desire is toward you.

Sometimes, seized by this desire, the Beloved takes matters into his own hands and commands the doors to the castle to be closed, even the outer walls. He wants to carry the soul away, and his ardor steals its breath. Teresa tells us that it is here that you can't speak. Your senses seem to fade. Your body may grow cold on the outside, but you won't feel it. You may look like you have physically died, but don't worry. This intense state is brief. When the suspension of the faculties passes, you will come back to yourself so nourished that you'll want to die again and thereby give more life to your happy, happy soul.

I know it sounds strange, and I can't emphasize enough how fleeting these states are. You may not notice it's happened at first; you'll only know you've been with the Lord, and that you've been deeply loved.

Okay, that's enough said about ecstasies or raptures. They're just too difficult to articulate. Besides, I've had precious little experience with them, and nothing lately except for a few shining instances after I take Communion. Teresa, however, more often lived on a higher plane than we pilgrims do. But that doesn't mean we can't aspire to have what she did.

"Come to the silence," my Beloved calls, again and again. The words wrap around me like a soft shawl. But I'm usually resisting, and I don't know why. Perhaps I still don't want to die to my attachments, yet more of Christ is on the other side of that surrender, so I long for it, too. Or maybe it's just hard to persevere, but not doing so is leaving me scattered and weary. Christ my lover is so compelling he makes me ache for him.

• • •

We have just one more stop now. I'll be more quiet there, to take it all in. Most of what you read will be Teresa's words, but surely you trust her by now. I'm just going to paraphrase them a bit, as I've been doing, and arrange them as if we're sitting in her parlor having the kind of conversation she had with John of the Cross.

As for me, I'm praying that I am given the mercy to go where Teresa has been, despite my failings. Really, who doesn't want to go to heaven? And I don't mean the one up in the sky.

Take it away, dear Teresa. You have our attention.

The Seventh Dwelling

"My dear friends, you may think that much has been said about the spiritual journey, and nothing can be added, but that would be a mistake. God's greatness has no limits; neither have his works. Who can finish telling of his mercies and grandeur?

"Each of us possesses a soul, but since we don't value them as being made in the image and likeness of God, we fail to understand the deep secrets that lie in them.

"May it please His Majesty to give me wisdom to say something of the many things he reveals to souls he leads into this mansion. I've begged him to help me, since he knows the only thing I want to do is tell you of his mercies, for the praise and glory of his name. I hope he will do this, not for me, but for you, friends, so that you will put no obstacle in the way of your soul's spiritual marriage to the Bridegroom, which brings, as you will see, so many blessings.

"When our Lord is pleased to take pity on the soul he has already taken as his spiritual bride because of our longing for him, he brings it, before the marriage is consummated, into his inner chamber, which is the seventh dwelling. For just as he does in heaven, His Majesty must have a room inside the soul where he alone dwells. Think of it as another heaven.

"In the seventh dwelling things are different from before. God removes the scales from the eyes of the soul so she can understand in some way the grace she's received. First she is illuminated by a cloud of magnificent splendor. After that, all three persons of the Blessed Trinity reveal themselves through a mysterious manifestation of the truth. All three divine persons are distinct, but through a sublime, infused knowledge, the truth that the three are of one substance, power, and knowledge, one God, permeates the soul. What we knew by faith is now understood by sight, so to speak. We don't see this with the eyes of the body, or even of the soul since this is not an imaginary vision. The most blessed Trinity communicates to the soul and makes it understand the words of the Gospel, where our Lord said that he, the Father, and the Holy Spirit will come to make their abode in the soul that loves God and keeps his commandments.

"You may think a soul who experienced this is so beside herself she—I'm using 'she' for now she is truly his bride—can't think about or do anything else. The truth is, she's more active than before, especially where God's work is concerned, and when she's not busy serving him, she enjoys his ceaseless companionship. Unless she turns away from God, he'll keep her aware of his presence and she'll possess an assurance that God will never take the favor he's given her away now that he's bestowed it. This inspired her more to never offend him in any way.

"When this happened to me, I found myself renewed in all the virtues. Whatever trials I experienced, or tasks I had to perform, the center of my soul never moved from its resting place. I began to think my soul was divided, and this troubled me. I complained to God about my love-struck soul the way Martha complained about Mary! It's just that my soul enjoyed such solitary peace, while the rest of me was full of troubles and preoccupations, and I couldn't keep it company. I know it sounds silly, but these things happen.

"But God begins to show us how much he loves us by revealing the vast reaches of his love. All he wants is to be joined with us so we can never be torn apart. In total union no separation is possible. The soul remains perpetually in that center with God. We could say that spiritual union is symbolized by two candles whose flames touch until they are one light. Or we could say that the wick, the wax, and the light all become one, but you can still separate the two candles again. Or the wick can be withdrawn from the wax.

"But spiritual marriage is like rain falling from heaven into a river or stream. They become a single body of water, where river and rainwater are impossible to separate. When a little stream flows into the ocean, who could separate it again?

"This center of the soul is difficult to explain. It's hard enough to believe it exists! I still can't come up with a good enough metaphor, but let me try.

"Think of a king, living in his palace. There may be all kinds of conflicts going on around him, but he remains inside come what may. Or think of this: our bodies can be hurt, but if our head feels fine, we're not going to get a headache. These metaphors are comical to me, friends. They make me laugh, but I can't think of any better. You can think what you want, but I'm telling you these things are true.

"O my friends, fix your minds on the Beloved; this is as it should be. Forget about yourself and dwell on how to please and love him better. This is the purpose of prayer. It is why the Beloved joins himself to us in marriage, and our children are always good works.

"The good works you do are an unmistakable sign that the favors you've received have come from God. What good would it do to be deeply recollected when I'm alone, acting virtuously and promising to perform wondrous works for God, but when the opportunity presents itself, I do the opposite. All our time with God should yield great good.

"Therefore take care to lay a firm foundation, not of prayer and contemplation alone, because unless you acquire virtues, your souls will not grow very tall. There are few things worse than making no progress. To stop is to go back. If you love, however, you will never be content to come to a standstill.

"This is what I want us to strive for—to offer our petitions and practice prayer, not simply for our own pleasure, but to strengthen us to serve God. Remember what I told you: both Mary and Martha must entertain our Lord and keep him as their guest. And they can't be so rude that they don't offer him food. How can Mary do this if all she does is sit at his feet, if her more practical sister doesn't help her?

"You can do so much by prayer; do it! Don't try to help the whole world, but mostly the people in the circle of your influence. Your work will be all the better because you're more connected to it. Don't ever think your humility and self-denial, your readiness to serve, and your fervent love will not inspire the people around you to become more virtuous. These are great works, and they please the Lord. Do whatever is in your power to do, and His Majesty will see your willingness to do still more and reward you as if you'd won a multitude of souls. And don't say the people around you are already good enough. That isn't your business. If you pray and they become even better, they'll please God more, and their prayers will be more helpful to their neighbors.

"I'll conclude with another bit of advice: don't build towers without a foundation, for our Lord doesn't care so much for the importance of our works, but for the love with which we do them. When we do all we can, His Majesty will give us more to do. If we don't grow weary, but during this short time that this life lasts—it may be shorter than you think—we give our Lord all the sacrifices we can, within and without, His Majesty will unite them with the sacrifices he made to the Father for us on the cross, so that even if our deeds are small, they will be made great by the amplitude of our love.

"May it please His Majesty, my friends, that we all meet together one day in the place where we will praise him without ceasing, forever and ever. Amen."

• • •

A Word After

I hope you enjoyed this spirited journey. My greatest hope is that Teresa's teachings ignite a burning desire in you to pray. They certainly fanned a flame in me. It is my sincere hope that if you were saint leary before reading this book, you are open now to the spiritual delights and wisdom our heavenly friends have to offer.

Finally, I want to leave you with a blessing from St. Teresa of Avila's autobiography that sums up exactly how I feel.

I thank you, fellow pilgrims, for traveling with Teresa and me. Lord, have mercy on me, a sinner, and may God grant you peace.

Closing Prayer of St. Teresa
(and me, too!)

May His Majesty always keep you in his hands and make you a great saint.

May the light of God's Spirit illuminate me, this miserable woman so lacking in humility, who's been so bold as to take on the task of putting such sublime things into words. And may it please the Lord that I have not made a mistake in writing this, although surely I have. I've always hoped that through me God would receive some praise. This is what I begged him for, for many years. Since I haven't offered him praise with my own actions, I've dared to offer this account to you as an example of his great mercy.

The Lord is all-powerful and can hear me if he wants. Hear me, Lord. Do not allow this soul to be lost, Your Majesty. You have employed so much ingenuity in so many different circumstances to save my soul over and over. You have pulled me back from the abyss and brought me home to you. For this I am so grateful.

Amen!

Acknowledgments

This has been a wonderful, life-changing, incredibly difficult project. My most sincere thanks go to God for giving me both the strength and the opportunity to do it. I'm grateful he moved my editor, Jon Sweeney, to give me this chance. I'd be remiss if I didn't thank Phyllis Tickle, too, for being such an inspiration to me. Wily Phyllis, she knew I wanted to impress Jon. I think she put in a few good words for me. I'm also immensely grateful to the entire team at Paraclete Press that made this project such a pleasure to work on. This is a dream come true for this ragamuffin.

At Mass last Sunday I was ushered to the back pew and seated, for the first time, beneath a stunning stained-glass window. I wondered during most of the celebration who the beautiful woman hovering over me was. Just after Communion I stole another look at her and noticed for the first time the quill pen and book in her hands. She was none other than St. Teresa of Avila, and I felt this was a little sign that I'd make it to "The End" after all, and that I should let nothing upset me. You taught me so much about prayer and loving God. Thank you, my wonderful new patron.

I couldn't do any writing without such a loving, supportive family, including my extended family. Thank you Burneys and Bandeles for your steadfast love—especially Ken—and for having more than your fair share of patience. I also want to thank my mothers, Latrecia Stone and Rutha Burney. Their encouragement urged me forward. The Mellons, Ken and Dee Dee, were instrumental in providing research materials for me. This book was enriched because of their generosity.

And speaking of generosity, I'm so blessed to have the encouragement and support of the Beloved Little Community members Will and Lisa Samson. Thank you for extraordinary grace— and Frau Lisa, thanks for putting a fire under me at the end of this journey.

My agent makes a lot of magic happen in my life; only it's not magic, it's the results of his hard work and advocacy. Thank you, Chip MacGregor, my gentle beast and dear friend, for all you do.

Thank you also, dear friends, who hold a sistah up in every book I write. I don't have to name you all. There are too many of you, but you know who you are. However, I'm especially grateful to Amy Heath, Terry Behimer, Evette Drouillard, Lisa Samson, Mary Griffith, Steve Parolini, and my sister Carly Smith, for allowing me to mention them in this book.

And finally, to my church family in Inkster, how I miss you; thank you, Marilynn Webb and Mr. John Shannon, for many joyful conversations, and Father Gary Morelli for your gentle encouragement. Many thanks to my sponsor and friend Natalie Hines for telling everyone she knows about my books, along with her sister and best friend Gail Monk, and thank you so, so much, Glenn and Jane O'Kray, for being my cheerleaders and wise guides.

The Lord bless and keep you.
May he show you his face and have mercy.
May he turn his countenance to you and give you peace.
The Lord bless you.

Notes

Epigraph

xi *"It's silly to think..."* Teresa of Avila, *The Collected Works of St. Teresa of Avila, Volume 2*, translated by Kieran Kavanaugh, OCD, and Otilio Rodriguez, OCD (Washington: ICS Publications, 1980) Prologue, 4, paraphrased by Claudia Mair Burney. Hereafter cited as "Teresa and Burney, *Interior Castle*," with part, chapter, and page number separated by periods.

Author's Note

xiii *"From silly devotions and sullen saints..."* Woodeene Koenig-Bricker, *Praying with the Saints: Making Their Prayers Your Own* (Chicago: Loyola Press, 2001), 220.

My Invitation and Yours

xvi *"Where have you hidden..."* Saint John of the Cross, *Saint John of the Cross: Selected Writings*, edited by Kiernan Kavanaugh, OCD (Mahwah, NJ: Paulist Press, 1987), 221.

xvii *"O you guiding night!"* John of the Cross, "The Dark Night: Stanzas of the Soul," in *The Collected Works of Saint John of the Cross*, rev. ed., translated by Kieran Kavanaugh, OCD, and Otilio Rodriguez, OCD (Washington: ICS Publications, 1991), stanza 5 (available online at www.karmel.at/ics/john/dn.html).

xvii *"Thanks be to God, daughters. I have found a friar and a half..."* E.A. Peers, *Spirit of Flame* (London: Sheed and Ward, 1943), 18–19.

xix *"Let nothing upset you. . ."* Teresa of Avila, *The Complete Poetry of St. Teresa of Avila: A Bilingual Edition*, translated by Eric W. Vogt (New Orleans: University Press of the South, 1996).

1 St. Teresa of Avila's Sparkling Life

4   *"Our reading romance novels…"*   Teresa of Avila, *The Collected Works of St. Teresa of Avila, Volume 1*, translated by Kieran Kavanaugh, OCD, and Otilio Rodriguez, OCD (Washington: ICS Publications, 1987), 2.1, paraphrased by Claudia Mair Burney. Hereafter cited as "Teresa and Burney, *The Book of Her Life*," with chapter and paragraph number separated by periods.

4   *"When I began to realize what I had lost…"*   Teresa and Burney, *The Book of Her Life*, 1.7.

4   *"I didn't think…"*   Teresa and Burney, *The Book of Her Life*, 2.1

4   *"I longed to please…"*   Teresa and Burney, *The Book of Her Life*, 2.2

6   *"It is interesting…"*   Alban Butler, *Butler's Lives of the Saints*, edited by Peter Doyle, 12 vols., October (Collegeville, MN: The Liturgical Press, 1996), 95.

8   *"My fondness for good books…"*   Teresa and Burney, *The Book of Her Life*, 3.7.

9   *"When I left my father's house…"*   Ibid., 4.1.

10   *"The Lord revealed to me how kind he is…"*   Ibid., 4.2.

11   *"I didn't know how to proceed in prayer…"*   Ibid., 4.7.

13–14   *"They administered the sacrament…"*   Ibid., 5.9

14   *"I had bitten my tongue to pieces…"*   Ibid., 6.1.

14   *"I suffered those years with gladness. . ."*   Ibid., 6.2.

15   *"This was the worst trick the devil…"*   Ibid., 7.1.

15   *"I loved that man so much…"*   Ibid., 7.14.

16   *"The sight of it utterly destroyed me…"*   Ibid., 9.1.

17   *"Since I couldn't seem to make reflections…"*   Ibid., 9.6.

17   *"It seemed to me that when he was alone and afflicted…"*   Ibid., 9.4.

17   *"I desired to wipe his brow…"*   Ibid., 9.4.

17–18   *"As I began to read the* Confessions*…"*   Ibid., 9.7.

18   *"One day while I was in prayer…"*   Ibid., 28.1.

18   *"he granted me the favor of seeing…"*   Ibid., 28.1.

19–20   *"Sometimes love, like an arrow…"*   Ibid., 29.10.

21   *"At that time the devil was preying…"*   Ibid., 23.2.

22–23   *"He started out determined to guide me…"*   Ibid., 23.8.

23   *"What I'm trying to say is that, though well meaning…"*   Ibid., 23.9.

24   *"Martha and Mary must…"*   Teresa and Burney, *Interior Castle*, 7.4.12.

25   *"When I fast I fast..."*   Tessa Bielecki, *Teresa of Avila: Ecstasy and Common Sense* (Boston: Shambhala Publications, 1996), 2.

25   *"By taking this road we gain . . ."*   Teresa of Avila, *The Way of Perfection*, translated by Henry L. Carrigan Jr. (Brewster, MA: Paraclete Press, 2009), 88.

25   *"If there is any way I can imitate..."*   Ibid., 108.

25   *"Only with that surety I will die..."*   Teresa of Avila, *The Collected Works of St. Teresa of Avila, Volume 3*, translated by Kieran Kavanaugh, OCD, and Otilio Rodriguez, OCD (Washington: ICS Publications, 1985), 376.

26   *"God be praised. They won't need..."*   Carol Lee Flinders, *Enduring Grace: Living Portraits of Seven Women Mystics* (New York: Harper Collins, 1993), 190.

26   *"My Lord, and my Bridegroom . . ."*   Tessa Bielecki, *Teresa of Avila: Mystical Writings* (New York: Crossroad Publishing, 1994), 26.

26   *"I am a daughter of the Church."* Ibid.

27-28   *"If this is how you treat your friends..."*   Koenig-Bricker, 219.

2 Exactly Where Are We Going?

29   *"We do not need wings to search..."*   Teresa and Carrigan, 116.

33   *"When I repeat the 'Our Father,' I think..."*   Ibid., 101.

34   *"It is called recollection because..."*   Ibid., 116.

35   *"like the whip used to start a top..."*   Francisco de Osuna, *The Third Spiritual Alphabet*, translated by Mary Giles (Mahwah, NJ: Paulist Press, 1981), 23.

36   *"I tried as hard as I could..."*   Teresa and Burney, *The Book of Her Life*, 4.7.

36–37   *"I have always been terrible at praying..."*   Mike Yaconelli, in *Ragamuffin Band, Ragamuffin Prayers*, edited by Jimmy Abegg (Eugene, OR: Harvest House Publishers, 2000), 44.

37   *"Books were my companions . . ."*   Teresa and Burney, *The Book of Her Life*, 4.9.

39   *"The Lord told me..."*   Ibid., 32.8.

39   *"How you begin is all important..."*   Teresa of Avila, *The Collected Works of St. Teresa of Avila, Volume 2*, translated by Kieran Kavanaugh, OCD, and Otilio Rodriguez, OCD (Washington: ICS Publications, 1980) 21.2, paraphrased by Claudia Mair Burney. Hereafter cited as "Teresa and Burney, *The Way of Perfection*," with chapter and paragraph number separated by periods.

40   *"His Majesty is the friend of courageous souls..."*   Teresa of Avila, *The Letters of Teresa of Jesus*, edited by E. Allison Peers, 2 vols., (Westminster, MD: Newman Press, 1950), 13.2 paraphrased by Claudia Mair Burney. Hereafter cited as "Teresa and Burney, *Letters*," with chapter and paragraph number separated by periods.

40   *"The greatest labor is in the beginning..."*   Teresa and Burney, *The Book of Her Life*, 11.5.

3 Make a Garden

41   *"The beginner must see himself as making a garden..."*   Teresa and Burney, *The Book of Her Life*, 11.6.

42   *"It seems to me I read or heard..."*   Ibid.

43–44   *"Now let's see how we need to water the garden..."*   Ibid., 11.7.

44   *"The four ways of watering the garden..."*   Ibid., 11.8.

44   *"Nothing I've found is more appropriate..."*   Teresa and Burney, *Interior Castle*, 4.2.2.

44   *"It'll even cool off large fires."*   Teresa and Carrigan, 76.

44–45   *"Do you know what cleansing properties there are . . ."*   Ibid., 78.

45   *"Thirst means the desire for something..."*   Ibid., 79.

4 Get to Know Yourself

47   *"We can say beginners in prayer are those..."*   Teresa and Burney, *The Book of Her Life*, 11.9.

49   *"It seems to me my soul is like a bird..."*   Teresa and Burney, *Interior Castle*, 4.7.15.

49   *"The imagination and memory can war with each other..."*   Teresa and Burney, *Letters*, 17.6.

49   *"The intellect is so wild it's like a frantic wild man..."*   Ibid., 30.12.

49   *"When, my God, will I see my soul..."* Ibid., 30.16.

50   *"We can say beginners in prayer are those..."*   Teresa and Burney, *The Book of Her Life*, 11.9.

50   *"On this journey there are no giant souls..."*   Ibid., 13.15.

51–52   *"The Sankofa symbol is most..."*   Harriette Cole, *Vows: The African-American Couple's Guide to Designing a Sacred Ceremony* (New York: Simon and Schuster, 2005), 18.

53   *"Humility is like a bee..."*   Teresa and Burney, *Interior Castle*, 1.2.8.

53   *"By gazing at his grandeur. . ."*   Ibid.

53-54 *"Oh, God, help me."*   Ibid., 2.11

54 *"The surest sign of repentance…"*   Teresa and Burney, *The Book of Her Life*, 11.9.

55 *"At that moment…"*   Quoted from the biography of Brennan Manning, found online at www.brennanmanning.com.

55 *"God grant that there is . . ."*   Teresa of Avila, *The Life of Saint Teresa of Jesus: Of the Order of Our Lady of Carmel*, translated by David Lewis, p. 98, paragraph 14, found online at www.forgottenbooks.org, paraphrased by Claudia Mair Burney.

5 Look for New Growth

59 *"It is important for you to realize…"*   Teresa and Carrigan, 94.

60 *"When you approach God…"*   Ibid., 95.

61–62 *"The Our Father à la St. Teresa in Ten Easy Steps"*   Ibid., 102.

62 *"If, while I am speaking with God . . ."*   Teresa and Henry L. Carrigan, 93.

64 *"What will these gardeners do if…"*   Teresa and Burney, *The Book of Her Life*, 11.10.

64 *"These labors take their toll. . ."*   Ibid.

64 *"God is so good that when for reasons…"*   Ibid., 11.9.

65 *"Pay no attention. . ."*   Teresa and Burney, *Letters*, 59.

66 *"Place yourself in the presence of Christ . . ."*   Teresa and Burney, *The Book of Her Life*, 13.11.

6 Cranking It Up!

67 *"I've explained how the gardener waters…"*   Teresa and Burney, *The Book of Her Life*, 14.1.

69 *"You would not be humble if God…"*   Teresa and Carrigan, 115.

70 *"I began to envy . . ."*   St. Teresa of Avila, *The Collected Works of St. Teresa of Avila, Volume 1*, translated by Kieran Kavanaugh, OCD, and Otilio Rodriguez, OCD (Washington: ICS Publications, 1987), paraphrased by Claudia Mair Burney, from *Spiritual Testimonies*, 39.1.

73 *"It is a state in which the soul enters…"*   Teresa and Carrigan, 128.

75 *"When His Majesty grants it, he does so…"*   Teresa and Burney, *Interior Castle*, 4.3.3.

75 *"He calls such people to give their attention…"*   Ibid.

75 *"If we desire to make room for His Majesty…"*   Ibid.

75 *"When you find yourself in this state of prayer…"*   Teresa and Carrigan, 133.

76 *"The sea voyage can be made…"*   Ibid., p. 117.

76 *"In this work of the spirit…"*   Teresa and Burney, *Interior Castle*, 4.3.5.

77 *"an accurate assessment of a true situation."*   Richard Foster, *Prayer: The Heart's True Home* (New York: Harper Collins, 1992), 27.

7 The Glorious Foolishness

83 *"Now let's speak about the third water that nourishes…"*   Teresa and Burney, *The Book of Her Life*, 16.1.

84 *"In this prayer, the faculties fall asleep . . ."*   Ibid.

84 *"I don't know any other way…"*   Ibid.

85 *"This person is like a man already holding…"*   Ibid.

88 *"Work that would take a poor soul twenty…"*   Ibid., 17.2.

90 *"A person utters innumerable praises…"*   Ibid., 16.4.

91 *"Contemplative prayer is considered to be…"*   Thomas Keating, *Informational Pamphlet on Centering Prayer*, found on the Contemplative Outreach Web site at www.contemplativeoutreach.org/ site/PageServer?pagename=about_practices_centering.

8 Holy Longing

97 *"Nothing compares to the delight…"*   Teresa and Burney, *The Book of Her Life*, 16.4.

99 *"While we are all equally precious in the eyes of God…"*   Foster, 156.

99–100 *"I can't persuade myself to use my human efforts…"*   Teresa and Burney, *Interior Castle*, 4.3.5.

100–01 *"Teresa's Four Reasons…"* Ibid. 4.3.

101 *"can also be Martha in such a way…"*   Teresa and Burney, *The Book of Her Life*, 17.5.

102 *"takes care of those less fortunate…"*   Ibid., 17.4.

102–03 *"How is this compatible…"*   Ibid., 37.8.

105 *"If he wants to bring the soul to…"*   Ibid., 17.2.

106 *"The soul is well aware that this is…"*   Teresa and Carrigan, 104.

107 *"My king, I beg you, make everyone I speak to…"*   Teresa and Burney, *The Book of Her Life*, 16.4.

9 Ecstasy Is Not a Drug

109 *"May the Lord give me the words..."*   Teresa and Burney, *The Book of Her Life*, 18.1.

109–10 *"In all the types of prayer that were explained..."*   Ibid.

110 *"One dark night, fired with love's urgent longings..."*   John of the Cross and Kavanaugh, 162.

113 *"The soul understands very well the sun's..."*   Teresa and Burney, *The Book of Her Life*, 18.12.

114 *"Once the faculties have begun to taste..."*   Ibid., 18.13.

114 *"The soul detaches itself from everything, daughter..."*   Ibid., 18.14.

114–15 *"All I can say is the soul appears to be joined..."*   Ibid.

116 *"My Lord, the only thing I ask for in life..."*   Teresa of Avila, *The Collected Works of St. Teresa of Avila, Volume 2*, translated by Kieran Kavanaugh, OCD, and Otilio Rodriguez, OCD (Washington: ICS Publications, 1980), *Meditations on the Song of Songs*, paraphrased by Claudia Mair Burney, 3.15.

10 The Door to the Castle

117 *"If you reflect carefully on this, my friends..."*   Teresa and Burney, *Interior Castle*, 1.1.1.

118 *"It came to me that the soul. . . "*   Ibid.

118 *Let's imagine there are many rooms in this castle..."*   Ibid., 1.1.3.

119 *"My understanding is that the entry door..."*   Ibid., 1.1.7.

120–21 *"They're like disabled people. . ."*   Teresa and Burney, *Interior Castle*, 1.8.1

11 Dwellings One, Two, and Three

127 *"It is very important for a soul..."*   Teresa and Burney, *Interior Castle*, 1.2.8.

129 *"Before I go on you should consider..."*   Teresa and Burney, *Interior Castle*, Ibid., 1.2.1.

130 *"O souls set free by the blood of Jesus Christ..."*   Ibid., 1.2.4.

131 *"Even though a soul may not be..."*   Ibid., 1.2.14.

131 *"Each one should do..."*   Ibid., 1.2.14.

132 *"There are many people who, because of their sins..."*   Ibid., 1.2.15.

134–35 *"Reason shows us that the soul is mistaken if..."*   Ibid., 2.1.4.

12 The Fourth Dwelling

139 *"Since these dwelling places…"* Teresa and Burney, *Interior Castle*, 4.1.2.

140 *"Without temptation, the devil could deceive us…"* Ibid., 4.1.3.

141–42 *"Consolations are those experiences…"* Ibid.

142 *"Spiritual sweetness begins in God…"* Ibid., 4.1.4.

143–44 *"The two fountains fill with water in different ways. . ."* Ibid., 4.2.3–5.

145 *"St. Teresa's Top Five Reasons…"* Ibid., 4.2.9.

146 *"We belong to God, my friends…"* Ibid., 4.2.10.

147 *"O my Lord and my God…"* Ibid., 4.2.6.

13 The Mysteries of the Bridal Chamber

149 *"If we gained nothing . . ."* Teresa and Burney, *Interior Castle*, 7.3.9.

152 *"There the happy couple stays…"* This ancient Jewish wedding feast model is derived from an article by Chuck Missler called "The Rapture, The Wedding Model," found online at www.watchmanbiblestudy.com/Articles/RaptureWeddingModel.htm, and "The Messiah and the Jewish Wedding," by Rabbi Ken in care of Yeshuat Yisrael, found online at http://www.yeshuatyisrael.com/ messiah_wedding%201.htm.

152 *"In the inner wine cellar…"* John of the Cross and Kavanaugh, 225.

153 *"How few of us prepare our souls so that the Lord…"* Teresa and Burney, *Interior Castle*, 5.1.2.

153 *"Whether we have little. . ."* Ibid., 5.1.3.

153–54 *"You must have heard about the marvelous way that silk is made. . ."* Ibid., 5.2.2.

154 *"Courage my friends. Let's be quick to do this work…"* Ibid., 5.2.6.

157 *"The comparison may be crude…"* Ibid., 5.4.2.

157 *"The soul's rendezvous…"* Ibid., 5.4.3.

157–58 *"Now the soul is fiercely determined…"* Ibid., 6.1.1.

158–59 *"We must be diligent, continuously praying…"* Ibid., 5.4.9.

160 *"I know this pain seems to pierce the very heart…"* Ibid., 6.2.4.

162–66 *"My dear friends, you may think that much has been…"* Ibid., 7.1–4.

About Paraclete Press

Who We Are

Paraclete Press is a publisher of books, recordings, and DVDs on Christian spirituality. Our publishing represents a full expression of Christian belief and practice—from Catholic to Evangelical, from Protestant to Orthodox.

We are the publishing arm of the Community of Jesus, an ecumenical monastic community in the Benedictine tradition. As such, we are uniquely positioned in the marketplace without connection to a large corporation and with informal relationships to many branches and denominations of faith.

What We Are Doing

Books

Paraclete publishes books that show the richness and depth of what it means to be Christian. Although Benedictine spirituality is at the heart of all that we do, we publish books that reflect the Christian experience across many cultures, time periods, and houses of worship. We publish books that nourish the vibrant life of the church and its people—books about spiritual practice, formation, history, ideas, and customs.

We have several different series, including the best-selling Living Library, Paraclete Essentials, and Paraclete Giants series of classic texts in contemporary English; A Voice from the Monastery—men and women monastics writing about living a spiritual life today; award-winning literary faith fiction and poetry; and the Active Prayer Series that brings creativity and liveliness to any life of prayer.

Recordings

From Gregorian chant to contemporary American choral works, our music recordings celebrate sacred choral music through the centuries. Paraclete distributes the recordings of the internationally acclaimed choir Gloriæ Dei Cantores, praised for their "rapt and fathomless spiritual intensity" by *American Record Guide*, and the Gloriæ Dei Cantores Schola, which specializes in the study and performance of Gregorian chant. Paraclete is also the exclusive North American distributor of the recordings of the Monastic Choir of St. Peter's Abbey in Solesmes, France, long considered to be a leading authority on Gregorian chant.

DVDs

Our DVDs offer spiritual help, healing, and biblical guidance for life issues: grief and loss, marriage, forgiveness, anger management, facing death, and spiritual formation.

Learn more about us at our Web site:
www.paracletepress.com, or call us toll-free at 1-800-451-5006.

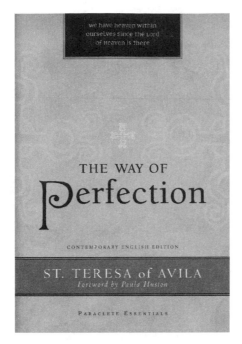

The Way of Perfection

TERESA OF AVILA

*"We have heaven within ourselves since the
Lord of heaven is there." —Teresa of Avila*

Teresa of Avila's warmhearted approach to Christian transformation will help you look deeply into what it means to know God and have a relationship with Jesus.

ISBN 978-1-55725-641-6 • TRADE PAPER, $15.99

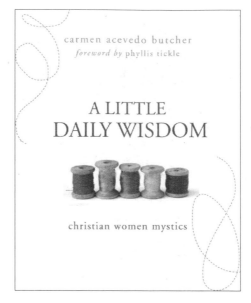

A Little Daily Wisdom
Christian Women Mystics
CARMEN ACEVEDO BUTCHER

"Remember kind actions—more than anything else–
cause the soul to shine with brilliance." —Gertrude the Great

Discover the strength, wisdom, and joyful faith of Christianity's legendary women—the medieval mystics. Their honesty and deep love for God will encourage and empower you every day of the year.

ISBN: 978-1-55725-586-0 • TRADE PAPER, $14.95